PROCEDURES FOR STRUCTURING AND SCHEDULING SPORTS TOURNAMENTS

Elimination, Consolation, Placement, and Round Robin Design

By

FRANCIS M. ROKOSZ

Director of Intramural – Recreational Play
Wichita State University
Wichita, Kansas

CHARLES C THOMAS • PUBLISHER

Springfield • Illinois • U.S.A.

Published and Distributed Throughout the World by
CHARLES C THOMAS • PUBLISHER
2600 South First Street, Springfield, Illinois, U.S.A.

© *1981 by* CHARLES C THOMAS • PUBLISHER
ISBN 0-398-04458-9
Library of Congress Catalog Card Number: 80-28994

*With THOMAS BOOKS careful attention is given to all details of
manufacturing and design. It is the Publisher's desire to present books that are
satisfactory as to their physical qualities and artistic possibilities and
appropriate for their particular use. THOMAS BOOKS will be true to those
laws of quality that assure a good name and good will.*

The material on pages 20-28, 43-59, 68-79, and 84 was substantially
reprinted from *Structured Intramurals* by Francis M. Rokosz. Copy-
right© 1975 by W. B. Saunders Company. Reprinted by permission
of Holt, Rinehart and Winston.

Printed in the United States of America
I - RX - 10

Library of Congress Cataloging in Publication Data

Rokosz, Francis M
    Procedures for structuring and scheduling sports
tournaments.

    Some material reprinted from the author's Structured
intramurals published in 1975.
    1. Sports — Organization and administration.
I. Title.
GV713.R64   371.8'9   80-28994
ISBN 0-398-04458-9

PREFACE

THE intent of this book is to give the reader a technical background in the structural design of sports tournaments, the mathematics attendant to their individual constructions, and the processes involved with scheduling people for play within particular tournaments.

Virtually all types of elimination, consolation, ladder, and round robin tournaments are discussed. In the first section, the reader learns, in step-by-step fashion, how the different types of tournaments work, what they can and cannot do, how to form them given any set of circumstances, the advantages and disadvantages of their use, and the calculations that can be made to determine such things as how long it will take to complete a tournament and how many play areas are required to do it.

The section on scheduling details the considerations on accepting entries for a tournament, the different forms schedules can take and how to formulate them, methods for communicating schedules to participants, how one determines who plays whom and when.

Some of what appears in this book has been taken from *Structured Intramurals* by Francis M. Rokosz, W. B. Saunders Company, Philadelphia, 1975. Permission to reprint has been obtained from Holt, Rinehart, and Winston. The discussion on tournaments and scheduling, which was originally presented in that book, has been substantially revised to offer a more understandable reading. Also, it must be noted that a good deal of the original work done in the area of tournament problem-solving can be attributed to C. M. "Dutch" Sykes, former Director of Campus Recreation at Pennsylvania State University. It was as his student and assistant that he stimulated me to expand upon his calculations, and to publish them for general consumption. I owe Dutch a great debt of gratitude for teaching me what he knows about the profession.

To Dutch, this book is thereby dedicated.

INTRODUCTION

A tournament is a formal and orderly system for impartially determining the winner of a competitive situation. It is structured in such a manner that all contestants are clearly identified and each has a theoretically equal chance of winning. Throughout the course of one's life, a person may periodically, or frequently, encounter competitive circumstances that require the formulation of a tournament. This book is intended to teach the reader how to construct and schedule a variety of tournaments in a variety of ways. It also discusses the factors that influence the selection of a particular tournament to satisfy a particular set of conditions or intentions. Consequently, the material is divided into two sections. Section I (Chapters 1-10) deals with tournament structure and the mathematics involved in solving problems attendant to the different structures. Section II (Chapters 11-16) details several methods by which contests can be scheduled within the given tournament structures.

Different tournaments have different features, of course, but all of them can be categorized as being one of four types: elimination, consolation, placement, or round robin. The first three chapters deal with elimination tournaments. As is indicated by their titles, they differ in structure and intent by eliminating entries from competition after one, two, or three losses. Instructions for bracket construction are given for each of the tournaments in their respective chapters, but the basis for all bracket constructions of all elimination, consolation, and placement tournaments is actually contained in the first chapter (Single Elimination Tournament). The principles of drawing a single elimination bracket are applied throughout most of the book, so the discussion is particularly detailed and important to understand.

All but a few of the other tournaments utilize a number of single elimination brackets, which may or may not be interconnected. For double and triple elimination tournaments, there are two and three interconnected brackets, respectively. That arrangement reflects the fact that an entry can incur a loss in the original bracket and be placed in a second or third bracket with other losers, all of which have a chance to win the tournament. For the consolation and placement tournaments (Chapters 5-8), there are two or more brackets, but none of them is connected with the others. That is the case because all brackets, other than the single elimination championship bracket, are designed to provide losers with additional competitive opportunities, even though no chance at winning the championship exists. The consolation brackets of a placement tournament take on the added significance of providing a method by which some or all of the entries' performances can be place-ranked, i.e. second-place finisher, third-place finisher, and so forth.

There are three tournaments that do not require brackets. The Continual Randomization Elimination Tournament (Chapter 4) is a structure that can be used to conduct single, double, and triple elimination tournaments, but its construction is much different. It does exactly what any of the other three tournaments do, but the structure allows its use for accomplishing certain administratively advantageous objectives. The Round Robin Tournament (Chapter 9) is different in concept from all the other tournament designs. No entry is eliminated from competition before any of the others, because each entry plays each other entry once. It is this type of structure (in conjunction with others) that is commonly utilized for team sports at all levels of competition. The Ladder Tournament, too, is different from all the other tournaments because its features allow one to employ it for several purposes. Realistically, it is a placement structure, since all entries are placed in separate positions from top to bottom; but the place rankings are necessarily liable to constant change, which does not happen with other placement structures.

Since each type of tournament arrives at a champion by a unique path, one must be aware of the relationships between the various tournament structures and the advantages and disadvantages of their use. There are many factors that influence the selection of a particular tournament to fit a particular set of conditions and intentions, and they are discussed in detail in Chapter 16. The tournament director must consider, for example, whether or not a tournament should be designed to give entries a chance to win the championship after having lost more than once, and if the entries should play the same number of contests.

Three of the major interrelated factors that ultimately determine the use or non-use of a tournament are (1) the number of entries, (2) the number of contests that can be conducted per time period, and (3) the total number of time periods available to conduct the tournament. For any tournament structure, large or small numbers of entries necessarily result in correspondingly large or small requirements in the number of time periods and/or the number of contests that can be conducted per time period. Similar relationships exist when each of the other two factors is increased or decreased. An absolute limitation on the number of time periods that can be used for a tournament might require the establishment of a corresponding limitation being placed on the number of entries that can be accommodated. It could also require an increase in the number of contests that can be played per time period (which is a function of the number of playing areas times the frequency of their use).

When one considers that, for any given number of entries, a double elimination tournament takes twice as long to run as does a single elimination, and a round robin usually takes longer to run than both of the others, it becomes important to be able to quickly determine, mathematically, which tournaments can be conducted under a given set of circumstances. Throughout the chapters on tournament structure, but particularly in those for single and double elimination and round robin (since they are the most frequently employed), calculations are presented that can aid the tournament director in making decisions on tournament selection. By establishing figures for any two of the above-mentioned factors, one can determine the numerical value of the third. For example, if it is known that ten contests can be played per day and, after the entry deadline, it is determined that there are sixty-five entries, then a tournament director can calculate the number of days it will take to arrive at a champion for a certain tournament structure, such as single elimination. The director can also determine the number of days required to run other types of tournaments, so he/she can weigh the possibilities. Furthermore, the director, for one reason or another, may have already decided upon the type of tournament to be utilized, and he/she may have to manipulate one of the factors to arrive at an acceptable situation. In the example just cited, assume that the number of days required to run the tournament turns out to be too high. What the director could do, in that event, is increase the number of contests that can be played per day, and that would reduce the number of days required.

All sorts of calculations and considerations are possible, and the advantage to knowing how to do the calculations is that determinations can be made within a minute or two; without the calculations, one would need to draw up the different tournament brackets and count out the number of days required to run the tournaments. Obviously, that is a time-consuming process; every effort should be made to understand and possibly memorize the calculations presented in each chapter.

Once the tournament director has gathered all the necessary information, has considered the factors involved, and has selected the appropriate tournament structure, the scheduling process can begin. Scheduling is a detailed plan on which the tournament can proceed in orderly fashion. A tournament schedule reveals to the reader who plays whom at what time on what day at what place. Chapters 11 through 14 describe, in step-by-step fashion, how a tournament schedule is produced from the taking of entries to the finished product. Since the most commonly used tournament structures are round robin and single and double elimination, procedures for their scheduling are illustrated; those procedures may be applied, with minimal adaptation, toward the scheduling of the other tournaments.

In Chapter 11, the reader learns how to establish policies and procedures for taking tournament entries. Several approaches are forwarded, and different types of entry forms are illustrated.

Chapters 12 and 13 give detailed accounts of how to produce single and double elimination schedules. Three types of schedules are discussed and each serves specific organizational and administrative purposes. For any tournament that is to take place indoors, the probability of having postponements is minimal; therefore, a printed schedule can be produced with specific dates, times, and playing areas designated for each contest. If postponements are a possibility, such as with outdoor events, then a schedule with dates and times listed would become meaningless upon the occurrence of the first postponement. To circumvent that problem, a type of schedule has been formulated that lends flexibility to the exact time a contest is to take place. A third type of schedule lists exact dates and times for each contest, but it does so in such a way that it can be used for certain outdoor sports.

Throughout all types of tournament schedules, procedures are shown for positioning entries on the bracket lines, indicating playing times, and providing other pertinent information. Further, directions and illustrations are given for utilizing worksheet brackets toward the eventual printing of a mimeographed schedule, which, in the case of a large number of entries, can involve a number of pages of standard size paper.

The schedules for round robin tournaments (Chapter 14) can take several forms, too. After it is determined how many leagues there will be and which entries are in which leagues, the tournament director must decide if he/she wishes to produce a schedule on which all teams in all leagues appear, or if just individual league schedules are to be published and communicated. Additionally, a factor such as entries' preferred playing times might influence a director to establish an instant scheduling procedure, which is described along with the more traditional approaches. Since most round robin structures involve a number of leagues, a playoff between league champions must be formulated to arrive at an overall champion. A variety of playoff systems exists, and the how and why of their structures and uses are thoroughly discussed.

On occasion, it may be desirable to establish a scheduling system whereby no champion is to be determined, and no two teams are scheduled against the exact same set of other teams. Random and Match-Up Scheduling Procedures (Chapter 15) are two systems that have been devised to accomplish that purpose. While the random method is suitable for a printed schedule, the match-up is designed for communication by other means, which allows for an avoidance of several disadvantages inherent in printing a schedule.

In effect, the reading and understanding of the contents of this book should prepare a person to handle virtually all tournament situations that may arise. A tournament director needs to know how to select a tournament, structure it, and schedule and publish it. Surely, some of the presented material will se_m complex and difficult to comprehend to some people, but a working knowledge of tournaments and scheduling can be obtained by just learning the basics, without learning absolutely everything in the book. Those who can go beyond the basics, and understand some of the finer points of tournament design and scheduling, will have the background to handle both simple and complicated circumstances with accuracy, efficiency, and confidence.

CONTENTS

PROCEDURES FOR STRUCTURING AND SCHEDULING SPORTS TOURNAMENTS

Section I

TOURNAMENT STRUCTURES
AND
PROBLEM-SOLVING

Chapter I
SINGLE ELIMINATION TOURNAMENT

BRACKET CONSTRUCTION

IN a single elimination tournament, entries (teams or individuals) are matched against each other in progressive fashion, such that the winner of a contest advances to the next round of play, and the loser is eliminated from further play. The tournament bracket (Fig. 1-1) consists of a number of horizontal lines, on which entries are placed one to each line in the first round. The lines are vertically connected to designate that entry A plays entry B, C plays D, and so forth. The lines are also connected horizontally in such a way that rounds of play, subsequent to the first, have exactly half the number of lines as the previous rounds. That corresponds to the concept that, for each contest played, one entry advances and the other is eliminated from the tournament.

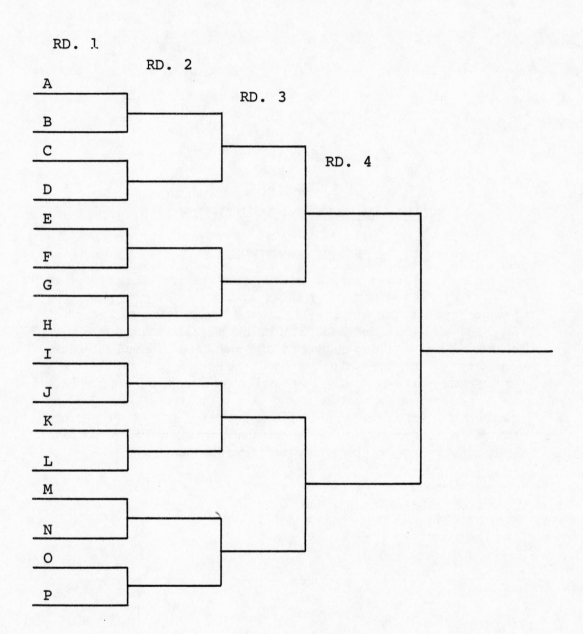

Figure 1-1.

A second bracket (Fig. 1-2) illustrates the progression of winners through the tournament. Entry E is the winner of the tournament, because it is the only entry that has not lost a contest, while all others have lost once. In a four-round tournament, Round 4 is called the "finals," Round 3 is the "semi-finals," and Round 2 is the "quarter-finals."

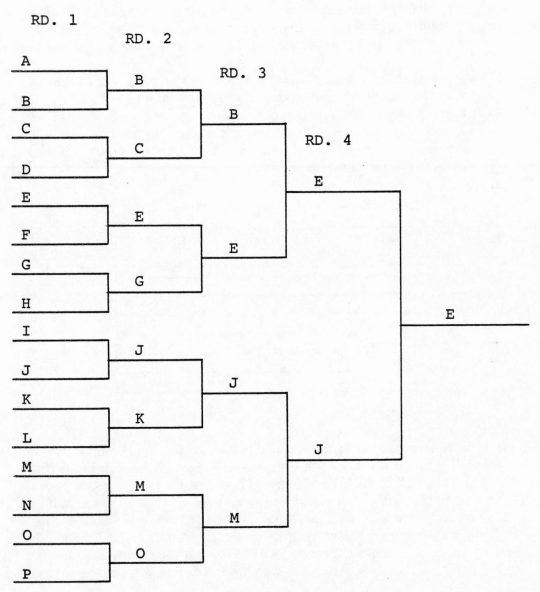

Figure 1-2.

The number of entries (16) used in the brackets thus far is what is known as a "power of two." Powers of two proceed as follows: 2, 4, 8, 16, 32, 64, etc. Whenever the number of entries in a tournament is a power of two, the number of lines in each round is a power of two, and each line in the first round is occupied by an entry. However, when the number of entries is something other than a power of two (21 for example), every line in the first round of the bracket is *not* occupied by an entry. Some entries must receive "byes," which means they do not play contests in the first round. They automatically advance to the second round of play, in which they play entries that advanced to the second round by virtue of winning a first-round contest.

The number of lines necessary for the formation of the first round of play, when the number of entries is not a power of two, is determined by the next higher power of two relative to the number of entries. The chart (Fig. 1-3) illustrates several relationships. The next higher power of two from 25 is 32, so the first round of the bracket contains thirty-two lines, the second round contains sixteen lines, and so forth.

NUMBER OF ENTRIES	NEXT HIGHER POWER OF TWO	NUMBER OF ROUNDS
2	2	1
3	4	2
6	8	3
14	16	4
25	32	5
51	64	6

Figure 1-3.

To demonstrate the formation of the bracket (Fig. 1-4), an example of thirteen entries is used. Note that sixteen lines must be available in the first round placement of the thirteen entries. Also note that three byes are placed on lines in the first round, such that the number of byes in the top half of the bracket approximately equals the number of byes in the bottom half. Further, byes should be evenly spaced throughout quarters and eighths of the bracket. Note that all byes are placed in the first round. From the second to final round, no byes occur, and each entry is paired with another entry.

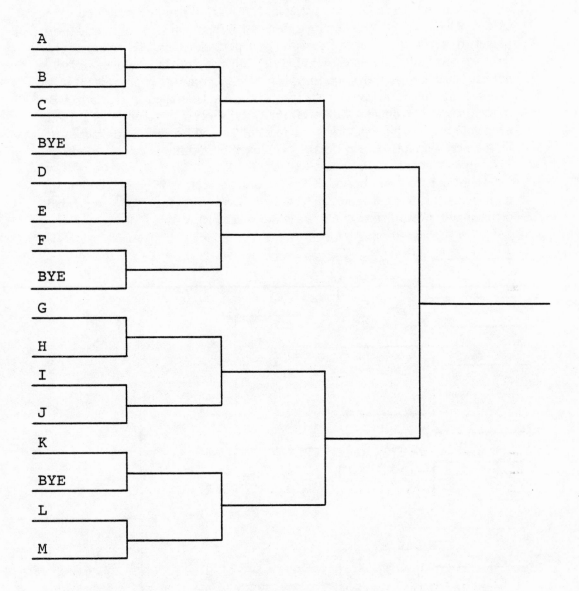

Figure 1-4.

The number of byes in a single elimination tournament can always be found by substracting the number of entries (N) from the next higher power of two. For example, when N = 23, the next higher power of two is 32; so, the number of byes equals 32 - 23, or 9. In equation form, it looks like this:

$$byes = NHPT - N$$
$$= 32 - 23$$
$$= 9$$

The correct placement of entries in the bracket can be just as important as the placement of byes. Quite often, a tournament director can identify players or teams that, on the basis of past performances, can be considered to have the best chances of winning the tournament. It would be unfortunate to have any of those top entries eliminated from the tournament in an early round due to inadvertent pairings of top entries against each other. By predicting which entries will perform most successfully, one can provide even competition by separating the top entries and preventing their meeting in the early rounds. The process by which that is done is called "seeding." The top entries are called "seeds."

There is no set number of seeds that must be placed in a bracket, but the number usually ranges from one to eight. The procedure for placing eight seeds in a bracket of sixteen entries is shown in Figure 1-5.

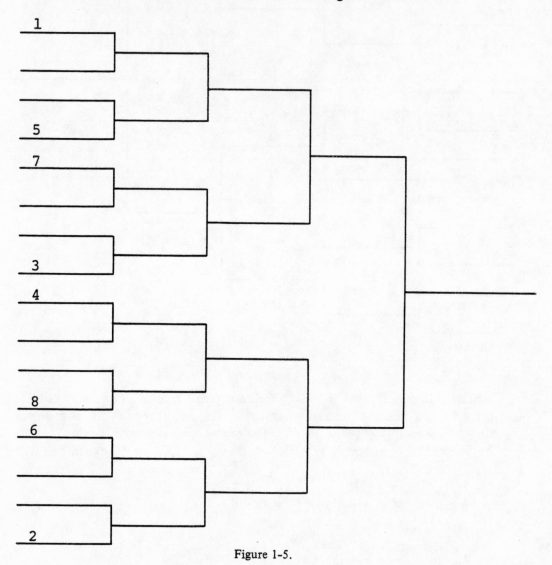

Figure 1-5.

Seeding proceeds by alternating placements in halves, and then quarters, of the bracket. The top seed is placed on the top line of the bracket, and the second seed is placed on the bottom line. The third seed goes on the bottom line of the upper half of the bracket, and the fourth seed goes on the top line of the lower half of the bracket. The fifth seed is placed on the bottom line of the upper quarter of the bracket, and the sixth seed is placed on the top line of the lower quarter of the bracket. The seventh seed goes on the top line of the second quarter of the bracket, and the eighth seed goes on the bottom line of the third quarter of the bracket. All other entries are placed by random draw.

A further consideration is the relationship of seeds to available byes. It is common practice to award byes to seeded teams in seeded order. So, if four byes are available, the first four seeds get them. There are at least two reasons why seeds get byes. For one, a bye is considered to be a reward for past performance. Second, the procedure allows a number of unseeded entries to play a first-round contest before having to meet one of the top seeds. That enhances the chances of unseeded entries to play more than one contest. A situation is illustrated (Fig. 1-6) where N = 11 and seven seeds can be identified. There are five byes, so the top five seeds get them.

Figure 1-6.

Thus far, the brackets have been drawn in a manner that clearly shows the placement of byes. However, brackets can be designed to save space by eliminating the word "bye" and the lines on which it appears.

All brackets can be broken down to smaller groups of twos, threes, and fours. The appropriate breakdown is achieved by continually halving the number of entries until a row of numbers appears in which threes are contained. There are only two possible combinations of numbers: threes and fours or threes and twos (Exception: when the number of entries is a power of two, the last row of numbers will contain only twos.) In the process, odd numbers are divided approximately. Two examples are shown.

N = 11	N = 29
11	29
6 – 5	15 – 14
3 – 3 – 3 – 2	8 – 7 – 7 – 7
	4 – 4 – 4 – 3 – 4 – 3 – 4 – 3

For eleven entries, the first and second rounds of the bracket (Fig. 1-7) are formed by drawing three 3s and one 2, in that order. Note that 2s are drawn as second round games. There are five byes, and the entries that receive them are placed on lines one through five. The bracket is completed by drawing and connecting the appropriate lines.

N = 11

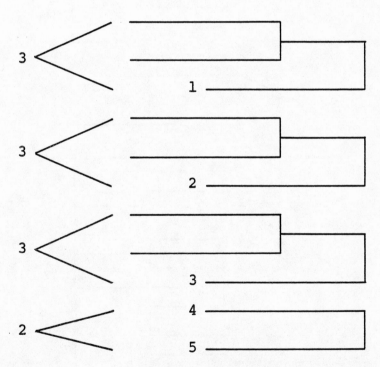

Figure 1-7.

For twenty-nine entries, the first and second rounds of the bracket (Fig. 1-8) are formed by drawing 4s and 3s, in the order indicated by the breakdown. Note that 4s are drawn as two first-round games. There are three byes, and the entries that receive them are placed on lines one through three. The bracket is completed by drawing and connecting the appropriate lines.

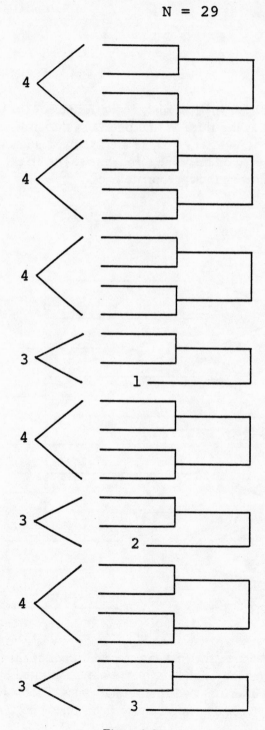

Figure 1-8.

Although the bracket design just described is basically sound, there is a problem that requires an adjustment. Remember that there are two stipulations for the placement of seeds and byes in a bracket. First, regardless of the size of the bracket, seeds must consistently appear on the same lines of the bracket; that is, the third seed is always placed on the last line of the upper half of the bracket. Consistency is required so one can identify seeded entries by virtue of the lines of the bracket on which they appear. Second, seeded entries must receive available byes in seeded order. A look at an example (Fig. 1-9) demonstrates the problem.

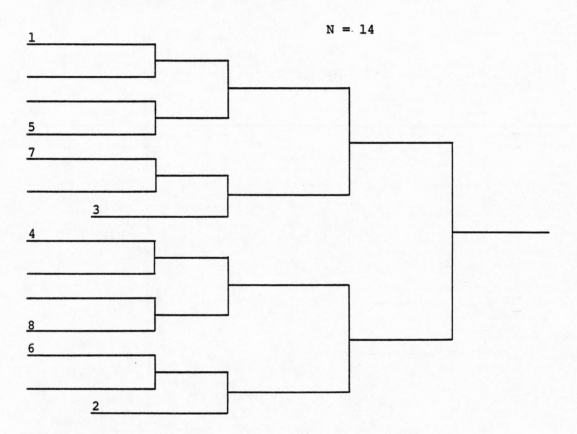

Figure 1-9.

If eight seeds are to be placed, they appear on the lines as shown. However, the bracket is drawn in such a manner that the two available byes are not given to seeds in seeded order. The top two seeds should get the byes, but the top seed plays a first-round game, while the second and third seeds get the byes. A system is required for correctly adjusting the bracket, and it is subsequently described.

A seeded single elimination bracket for twenty-seven entries is formed in the following steps and is illustrated in Figure 1-10.

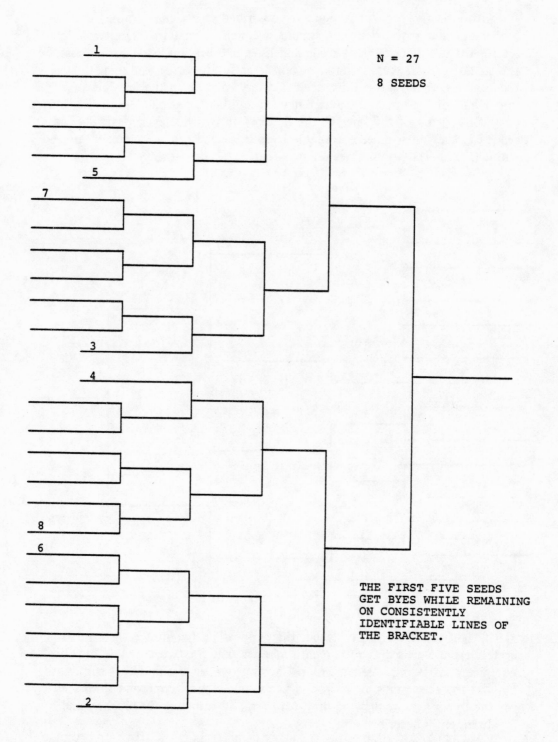

N = 27

8 SEEDS

THE FIRST FIVE SEEDS
GET BYES WHILE REMAINING
ON CONSISTENTLY
IDENTIFIABLE LINES OF
THE BRACKET.

Figure 1-10.

Step 1: Break down N until the appropriate numbers are reached.

$$27$$
$$14 - 13$$
$$7 - 7 - 7 - 6$$
$$4 - 3 - 4 - 3 - 4 - 3 - 3 - 3$$

Step 2: For reference purposes, designate quarters of the bracket by marking through the appropriate dashes.

$$4 - 3 + 4 - 3 + 4 - 3 + 3 - 3$$

Step 3: There are five byes in the bracket, and each "three" contains one. Since seeds are to receive byes in seeded order, the threes must be rearranged to correspond with the location of the first five seeds. The top seed is located in the first eighth of the bracket, so a 1 is placed in that spot. The second seed is located in the last eighth of the bracket, so a 2 is placed in that spot. The process is continued for five seeds.

$$4 - 3 + 4 - 3 + 4 - 3 + 3 - 3$$

$$1 \quad 5 \qquad 3 \quad 4 \qquad\qquad 2$$

Step 4: Threes are placed under the seeded spots, and the fours are filled in the remaining places.

$$4 - 3 + 4 - 3 + 4 - 3 + 3 - 3$$

$$1 \quad 5 \qquad 3 \quad 4 \qquad\qquad 2$$

$$3 \quad 3 \quad 4 \quad 3 \quad 3 \quad 4 \quad 4 \quad 3$$

Step 5: The bracket is formed in the adjusted order, with one further alteration. Whenever a three occurs in an odd-numbered portion (eighth, in this case) of the bracket, i.e. first, third, fifth, and so forth, it is drawn with the second round line above the two lines that form the first-round game (see below).

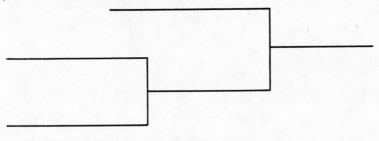

Structure 1

For threes that occur in even-numbered portions of the bracket, the draw is made with the second-round line below the first-round game (see below).

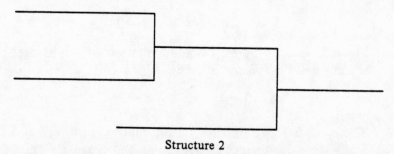

Structure 2

A slightly different situation occurs when the final lines of the entry breakdown result in twos and threes. A bracket for nineteen entries is shown in Figure 1-11.

$$
\begin{array}{c}
19 \\
10-9 \\
5-5-5-4 \\
3-2+3-2+3-2+2-2 \\
\hline
\end{array}
$$

1   3   2

_____

3   2   2   3   2   2   2   3

N = 19

8 SEEDS

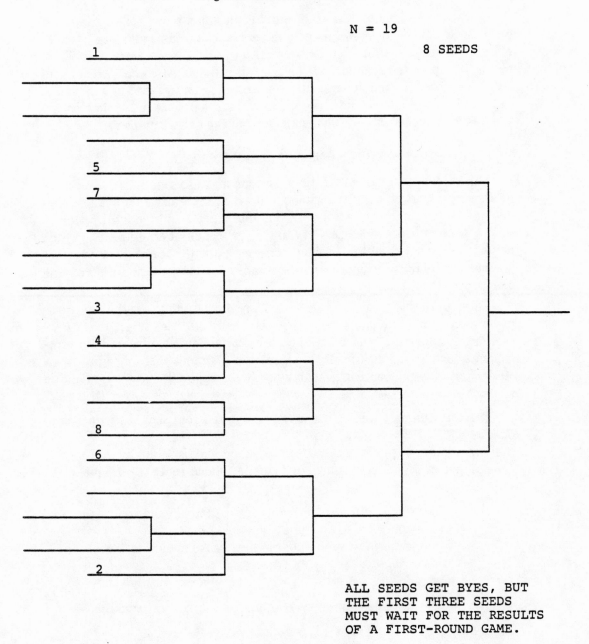

ALL SEEDS GET BYES, BUT
THE FIRST THREE SEEDS
MUST WAIT FOR THE RESULTS
OF A FIRST-ROUND GAME.

Figure 1-11.

Since a 2 designates a second-round game, thus a bye for both entries, one may wonder why the order of numbers (above) must still be adjusted to place 3s in seeded order. If that were not done, unseeded entries would be required to play the second and third seeds in their first contests. That situation is avoided by the adjustment, and unseeded entries can only be paired against the fourth seed and beyond. In effect, the procedure enhances the chances of unseeded entries advancing beyond their first contests.

TOURNAMENT PROBLEM-SOLVING

This section involves calculations one can make to determine, in advance of drawing a bracket, the circumstances in which the tournament can be conducted. There are three factors, or variables, that require consideration in solving tournament problems. They are (1) N, the number of entries, (2) the number of days needed to run the tournament, and (3) the number of games available for play each day. By predetermining any two of the variables, one can solve for the third.

All solutions to problems are based on the assumptions that no postponements are possible, and no entry plays more than once per day. However, any time period may be applied. For certain types of short-term tournaments, one might assume that no entry plays more than once per hour. Moderately fatiguing activities such as table tennis, pool, and chess might be applicable to that situation.

Three preliminary determinations are required for use in subsequent calculations.

The number of games that can be played per day is found by multiplying the number of play areas (courts or fields) available times the frequency of their use.

> *Example:* three courts are available for basketball, and four sessions of
> games are to be played on each court.
> games/day = number of courts x frequency of use
> $$= 3 \times 4$$
> $$= 12$$

The number of games in a single elimination tournament equals N −1.

> *Example:*　　　　　N = 15
> games　　= N - 1
> 　　　　　= 15 - 1
> 　　　　　= 14

The number of first-round games in the tournament equals N - (next lower power of two). That is true except when the number of entries is a power of two. The number of first-round games then equals N divided by 2.

Example: N = 23   Next lower power of two = 16
first-round games = N - 16
= 23 - 16
= 7

Problem Type I

Knowing the number of entries and the number of games that can be played each day, determine the minimum number of days required to run the tournament.

Example 1

Known: N = 27 and games/ day = 5

Step 1: Determine the number of first-round games.
first-round games = N - lower power of two
= 27 - 16
= 11

Step 2: Set up the number of rounds and the number of games for each round. When the number for first-round games has been appropriately designated, start with the last round (one game) and work backward with multiples of two.

round	1	2	3	4	5
games	11	8	4	2	1

Step 3: Determine the number of days needed to play round by round. Start with the last round and work backward. Eliminate those rounds that obviously take only one day to play (when the games per day are greater than, or equal to, the number of games in a round, place a 1 under that round).

round	1	2	3	4	5
games	11	8	4	2	1
days			1	1	1

Note: These are not necessarily the only rounds that can be played in one day. Also, because an entry cannot play more than once per day, no two full rounds can be played in one day.

Step 4: Start with the first round and determine the number of days required to play each round.

There are eleven first-round games, and five games can be played per day. Therefore, three days are required to play the first round. Since a total of 15 games could be played in three days, four possible games remain that can be used for games in the second round.

round	1	2	3	4	5
games	11	8	4	2	1
		−4			
		4			
days	3		1	1	1

Four games remain in round 2, and they require one day to complete.

round	1	2	3	4	5
games	11	8	4	2	1
		−4			
		4			
days	3	1	1	1	1

The total number of days required to run the tournament is determined by adding the numbers in the last line horizontally.

Answer: seven days

Example 2

Known: N = 17 and games/day = 9

Step 1: First-round games   = 17 - 16
                                  = 1

Step 2:

round	1	2	3	4	5
games	1	8	4	2	1

Step 3: Since nine games per day are available, each round can be played in one day.

round	1	2	3	4	5
games	1	8	4	2	1
days	1	1	1	1	1

Answer: five days

Note again that no two full rounds (for instance, the first and second rounds) can be combined for play in one day. This would necessitate the play of one entry twice in one day. Also note that a single elimination tournament can be run in a minimum number of days when the games available per day equal, or exceed, the number of games in the largest round. The minimum number of days is always equal to the number of rounds in the tournament.

Example 3

Three tournaments are to be run simultaneously.
Known: N = 36, 25, 14 and games/day = 6

Step 1: Determine the number of first-round games for each tournament.

$$\text{first-round games} = 36 - 32$$
$$= 4$$
$$\text{first-round games} = 25 - 16$$
$$= 9$$
$$\text{first-round games} = 14 - 8$$
$$= 6$$

Step 2: Set up the number of rounds and games for each round of each tournament. Add vertically to arrive at the total number of games in each round.

round	1	2	3	4	5	6
N = 36 games	4	16	8	4	2	1
N = 25 games		9	8	4	2	1
N = 14 games			6	4	2	1
total games	4	25	22	12	6	3

Step 3: With six games available for play each day, eliminate as many final rounds as possible.

round	1	2	3	4	5	6
total games	4	25	22	12	6	3
days					1	1

Step 4: Start with the first round and eliminate the remaining rounds.

round	1	2	3	4	5	6
total games	4	25	22	12	6	3
		-2	-1	-3		
		23	21	9		
days	1	4	4	2	1	1

Note: Care must be taken to avoid scheduling entries for play more than once per day. There are a very few situations where the use of a large number of games per day leads to an inaccurate answer. While assigning days to play games, look at the total set-up (in Step 2) to check that no entry is being scheduled more than once per day.

Answer: thirteen days

Problem Type II

Knowing the number of entries and the number of days available to run the tournament, determine the minimum number of games that must be available per day to run the tournament.

Example 1

Known: N = 39 and 6 days

Step 1: Establish the number of rounds and the number of games in each round.

round	1	2	3	4	5	6
games	7	16	8	4	2	1

Step 2: Divide the number of days available (6) into the number of games in the tournament (N - 1 = 38). This operation results in the first index number, which is 7 (always round off to the higher number). Working backward from the last round, recognize those rounds whose number of games is less than the index number 7. These rounds can be played in one day.

round	1	2	3	4	5	6
games	7	16	8	4	2	1
days				1	1	1

Step 3: Three days have been used to play the last seven games. Divide the remaining number of days (3) into the remaining number of games (31). The result is the second index number, which is 11. Still working backward, recognize those rounds whose number of games is less than 11. One day is required to play each of these rounds. Note that round 2 cannot be circumvented to get to round 1.

round	1	2	3	4	5	6
games	7	16	8	4	2	1
days			1	1	1	1

Step 4: Four days have been used to play the last 15 games. Divide the remaining number of days (2) into the remaining number of games (23). The third index number is 12. Twelve is smaller than the number of games (16) in round two. When this occurs, the index number becomes the answer to the problem.

Answer: twelve games per day

Example 2

Known: N = 34 and 5 days

Step 1: Establish the rounds and the number of games in each round.

round 1 2 3 4 5 6

The solution to the problem can be halted with the determination of the number of rounds in the tournament. Six rounds cannot be played in five days without having entries play more than once per day. At least six days are required. Therefore, there is no solution to the problem.

Example 3

Known: N = 39 and x days, where x represents the minimum number of days required to run the tournament with an unlimited number of games/day.

Step 1: Determine the number of games in the first and second rounds of the tournament.

$$\text{first-round games} = 39 - 32$$
$$= 7$$
$$\text{second-round games} = 32/2$$
$$= 16$$

Step 2: Add the first- and second-round games and divide by two to find the required games per day (this procedure holds when there are fewer first-round games than second-round games).

$$7 + 16 = 23$$

$$23/2 = 11\frac{1}{2} \quad \text{round off to higher number}$$

Answer: twelve games/day. Note: when the number of first-round games is greater than or equal to the number of second-round games, the required games per day is equal to the number of games in the first round. For example, if N = 14, there are 6 first-round games and 4 second-round games, so six games per day are required to run the tournament in the minimum number of days.

Problem Type III

Knowing the number of days available to run the tournament and the number of games that can be played per day, what is the maximum number of entries that can be taken?

Example 1

Known: 5 days and 9 games/day

Step 1: Multiply the number of available days (5) times the number of games that can be played each day (9).

$$9 \times 5 = 45$$

This represents the total number of possible games that could be played under the given conditions.

Step 2: Set up the maximum number of rounds and the maximum number of games for each round. The maximum number of rounds is always equal to the number of days available.

round	1	2	3	4	5
maximum games	16	8	4	2	1

Step 3: Nine games can be played each round. Working backward from round five, determine the number of wasted games in each round by subtracting from nine the maximum number of games for each round. When the maximum number of games for a round exceeds or equals the number of games that can be played per day, a 0 is recorded in the wasted games column.

round	1	2	3	4	5
maximum games	16	8	4	2	1
wasted games	0	1	5	7	8

total games wasted = 21

Step 4: Subtract the total wasted games (21) from the total possible games that could be played within the set restrictions (45).

$$45 - 21 = 24$$

This represents the maximum number of games that can actually be played in the tournament.

Step 5: The number of entries that can be accommodated is determined by setting up the appropriate formula.

$$\text{number of games} = N - 1$$
$$24 = N - 1$$
$$1 + 24 = N$$
$$25 = N$$

Answer: twenty-five entries

Example 2

Known: 20 days and 7 games/day

Step 1: Total possible games = days × games/day
$$= 20 \times 7$$
$$= 140$$

Step 2: Since a large number of days is available, it is more efficient to work backward, thus avoiding the need to set up all the rounds. With only seven games available per day, one can quickly identify the few final rounds that produce wasted games.

round	17	18	19	20
maximum games	8	4	2	1
wasted games	0	3	5	6

total games wasted = 14

Step 3: Tournament games = total games - wasted games

$$= 140 - 14$$

$$= 126$$

Step 4: Number of games = N - 1

$$126 = N - 1$$

$$1 + 126 = N$$

$$127 = N$$

Answer: 127 entries

Chapter II
DOUBLE ELIMINATION TOURNAMENT

BRACKET CONSTRUCTION

ESSENTIALLY, a double elimination tournament consists of two simultaneously operating single elimination tournaments that are connected by the matching of the winners of both brackets in a final contest or two. To begin the tournament, all entries play at least one contest in the upper single elimination bracket. Once an entry loses a contest in the upper bracket, it is placed in an appropriate section of the lower bracket. When an entry loses a contest in the lower bracket, it is removed from further participation. Thus, each entry is guaranteed the playing of a minimum of two contests, and two losses eliminate it from the tournament. The winner of the tournament is the entry that has lost one or no contests while all other entries have lost twice.

The construction of the upper bracket of the tournament is performed as it would be for a single elimination tournament of an equal number of entries. The upper bracket (Fig. 2-1) is drawn for sixteen entries, and the games are numbered sequentially. Since there are fifteen games in the bracket, there will be, as the tournament proceeds, fifteen losers to be placed in the lower bracket.

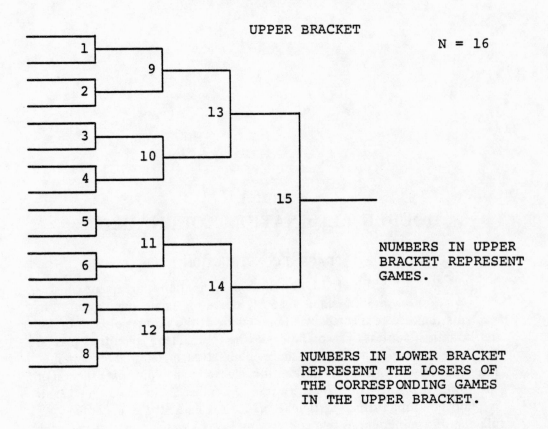

UPPER BRACKET

N = 16

NUMBERS IN UPPER
BRACKET REPRESENT
GAMES.

NUMBERS IN LOWER BRACKET
REPRESENT THE LOSERS OF
THE CORRESPONDING GAMES
IN THE UPPER BRACKET.

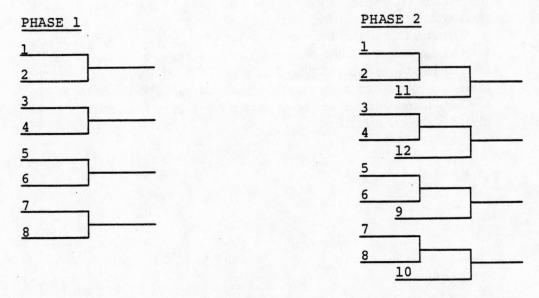

Figure 2-1.

PHASE 3

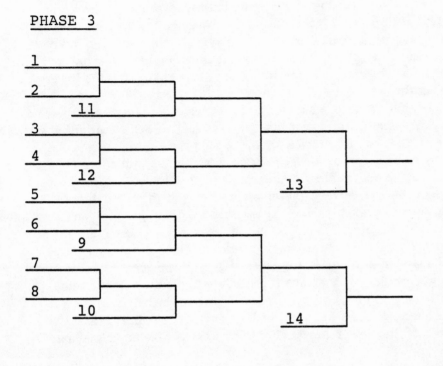

PHASE 4

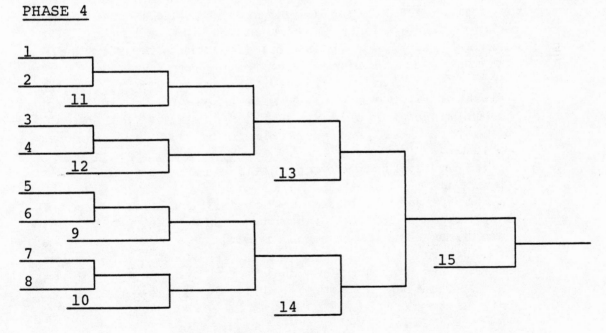

Figure 2-1. (continued)

There are eight games in the first round of the upper bracket which, when played, result in eight losers and four first-round games in the lower bracket. Phase 1 of the lower bracket shows the placement of the eight losers on the t racket lines in numerical order. The playing of the second round of the upper bracket results in four losers. Four lines in the lower bracket must be found on which to add the four losers, and Phase 1 of the lower bracket provides them.

From the second round onward, the order of placement of the numbers of upper bracket losers in the lower bracket is subject to being rearranged, such that the meeting of two entries for the second time in the tournament is delayed for as long as possible. Upper bracket numbers in the second round must be compared to their counterparts in the first round, so those numbers may be separated when placement is made in the lower bracket. For instance, upper bracket game 9 is a direct result of games 1 and 2; therefore, the loser of game 9 is placed in the lower bracket at a point that delays the meeting of the contestants of games 1 and 2 for as long as possible. As illustrated in Phase 2, the loser of game 9 is placed in the lower half of the lower bracket. It is standard procedure to place all second-round losers of the upper half of the upper bracket in the lower half of the lower bracket and all second-round losers of the lower half of the upper bracket in the upper half of the lower bracket. That process is illustrated in Phase 2.

The playing of the third round of the upper bracket results in two losers for which slots must be found in the lower bracket. Phase 2 of the lower bracket shows four lines; so, two games in the lower bracket must be played before the third-round upper bracket losers (13 and 14) can be inserted. The numerical order of their placement in the lower bracket depends on the relationships to their corresponding second-round games. Game 13 is a result of games 9 and 10, and game 14 is a result of games 11 and 12. Thus, the loser of game 13 is placed in that half of the lower bracket that does not contain the losers from games 9 and 10. In this case, that is the upper half. Naturally, the loser of game 14 is placed in the lower half. Phase 3 illustrates the process.

The final upper bracket loser remains to be inserted, and Phase 4 shows the placement. ·

The upper and lower brackets are connected (Fig. 2-2) so the winners of both brackets play each other. If the winner of the upper bracket defeats the lower bracket winner, the tournament is over because all but one entry has two losses. However, should the lower bracket winner defeat the upper bracket winner, both entries have one loss each, and one more contest is required, which is indicated by the dotted lines. The winner of the final contest is the champion.

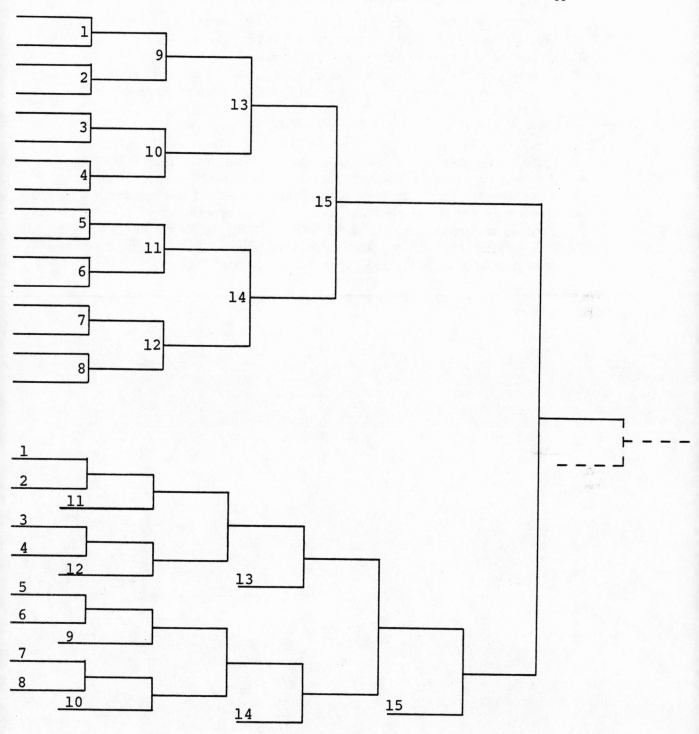

Figure 2-2.

Bracket construction for any number of entries that is not a power of two requires a slightly different procedure than previously described. The process for ten entries is subsequently explained.

Whenever the number of entries is not a power of two, the first two rounds of the lower bracket are immediately formed from the losers of the first two rounds of the upper bracket. The first two rounds of the upper bracket contain six games, so Phase 1 of the lower bracket contains six lines on which to place the losers. Phase 2 shows the placement of the first-round losers. Note that the loser of game 1 is placed in the upper half of the lower bracket, and the loser of game 2 is placed in the lower half of the lower bracket. That is the case because the placement of first-round losers always corresponds to their original position in the upper bracket, as it relates to eighths, quarters, or halves of the bracket. So, the placement of the loser of game 1 in the top half of the lower bracket corresponds to the original location of game 1 in the upper half of the upper bracket.

PHASE 1

PHASE 2

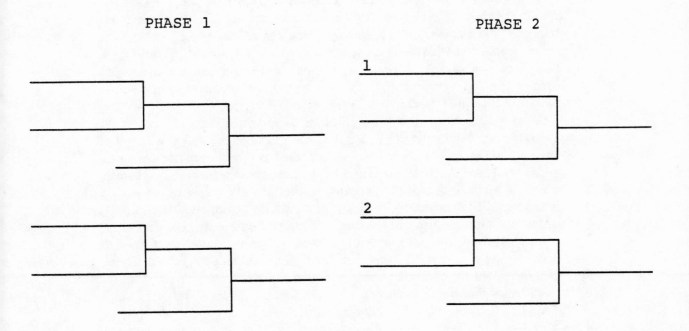

PHASE 3

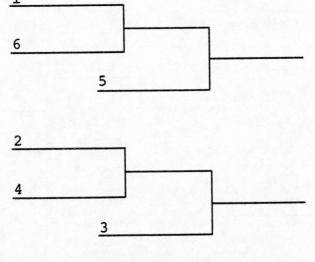

Structures 3, 4 and 5

Phase 3 shows the placement of game losers 3 and 4 in the lower half of the lower bracket, and game losers 5 and 6 in the upper half of the lower bracket. Note their exact placement. Since game 5 in the upper bracket cannot possibly be played until a game in the first round is played (game 2), the loser of game 5 is given the bye position in the lower bracket. The loser of game 6 is placed in the first round of the lower bracket because game 6 in the upper bracket can be played without waiting for a first-round game to be played. The advantage of that procedure is that if one could schedule four games per day, games 1, 2, 4, and 6 of the upper bracket could be played in the first time period. Because the losers of those four games comprise the first two games of the lower bracket, those two games, as well as games 3 and 5 of the upper bracket, can be played in the second time period. That makes for the most efficient use of time and facilities. If, for instance, the positions of the losers of games 5 and 6 in the lower bracket were reversed, the corresponding first-round game in the lower bracket could not be played until game 5 in the upper bracket were played. Therefore, the flow of the tournament would be delayed.

Phase 4 shows the placements of the losers of games 7 and 8. Since game 7 in the upper bracket is a direct result of games 3 and 4, the loser of game 7 must be separated, in the lower bracket, from the losers of games 3 and 4. Similar reasoning applies to the placement of the game 8 loser.

PHASE 4

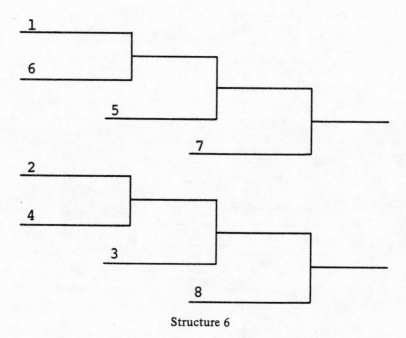

Structure 6

The placement of the final upper bracket loser, and the final bracket draw, are illustrated in Figure 2-3.

Another example (N = 15) is shown in Figure 2-4. Take particular notice of the placements of the upper bracket losers of games 1, 2, and 3. Game 1 of the upper bracket appears in the second eighth of the bracket, so its placement in the lower bracket is in the second eighth, as well. The locations of games 2 and 3 are the third and fourth eighths of both brackets, respectively. Note that, in some cases, a single line of the bracket can be considered an eighth of the bracket.

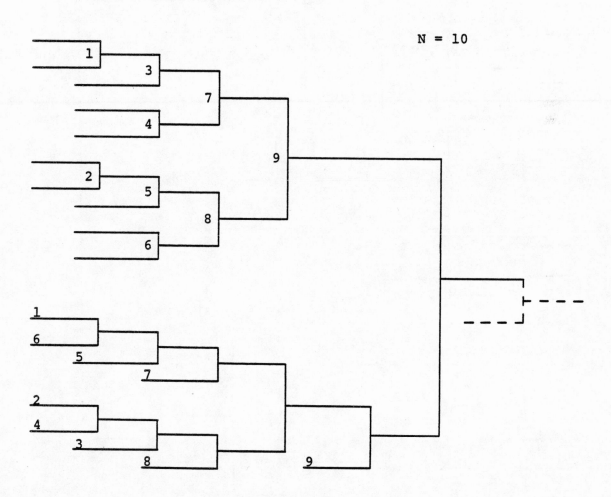

Figure 2-3.

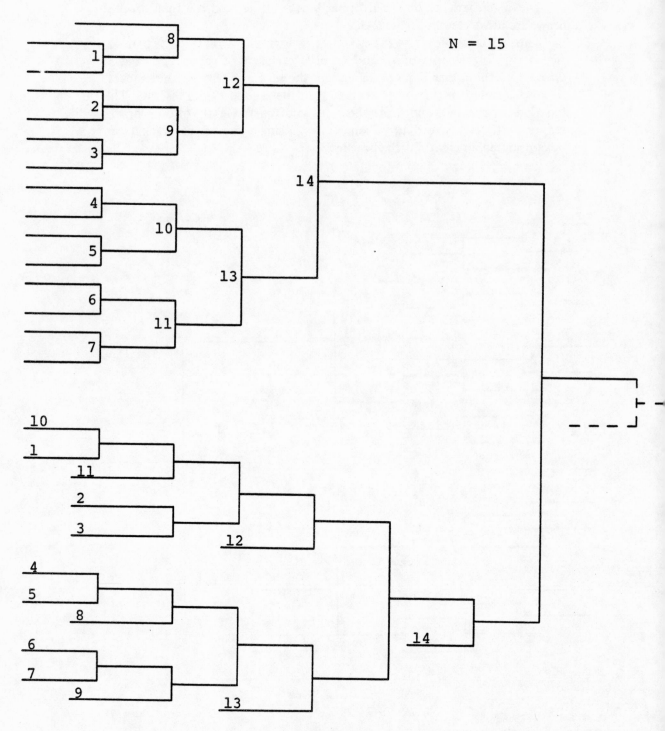

Figure 2-4.

Also note that, since the first two rounds of the upper bracket contain eleven games, the first two rounds of the lower bracket are constructed with eleven lines. The normal breakdown would have the upper half of the lower bracket constructed with six lines, and the lower half constructed with five. However, the number of lines in each half of the lower bracket must match the number of games (first two rounds) in the corresponding halves of the upper bracket. Therefore, the upper half of the lower bracket must contain five lines.

A more complex situation (N = 23) is shown in Figure 2-5. Note the placement of first-round losers. Eighths of the bracket are involved. The circled areas represent the fifth eighth of each bracket. Also notice the placements of the losers of upper bracket games 16, 17, 18, and 19. Game 16 results from games 8 and 9, the losers of which are placed in the lower half of the lower bracket. Therefore, the loser of game 16 must be placed in the upper half of the lower bracket. A further adjustment can be made by referring back to the first round of the upper bracket. Game 16 not only results from games 8 and 9. Initially, games 1 and 2 were involved; so, in the placement of the loser of game 16, the possible avoidance of the games 1 and 2 losers in the lower bracket must be considered. Thus, the game 16 loser, as well as losers for games 17, 18, and 19, is placed as shown.

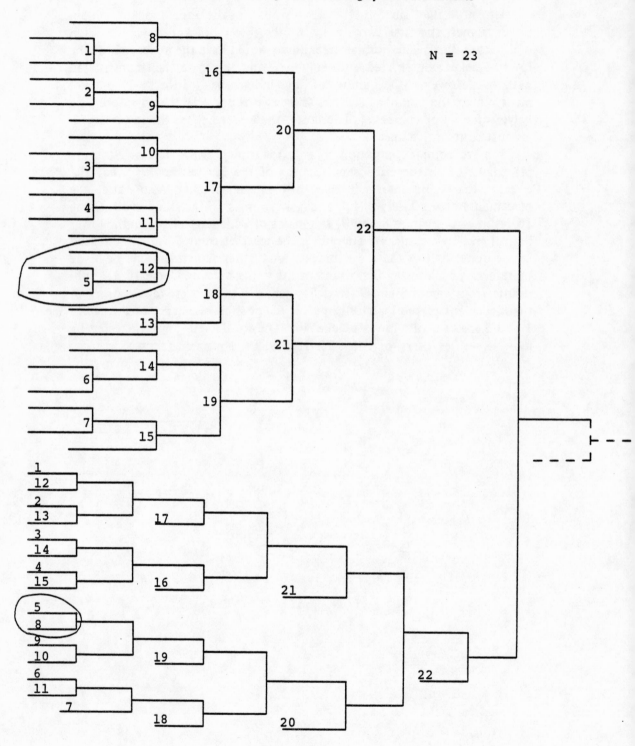

N = 23

Figure 2-5.

Summary of Bracket Construction for Non-Powers of Two

Determine the number of games in the first two rounds of the upper bracket, and construct the first two rounds of the lower bracket with that number of lines. The number of lines in the upper half of the lower bracket must equal the number of games (in the first two rounds) in the upper half of the upper bracket. The same is true for the lower halves of each bracket.

Upper bracket first-round losers are placed in the lower bracket, such that their relative positions in eighths, quarters, and halves of the brackets remain consistent. For example, if game 3 is in the third "eighth" of the upper bracket, the placement of the game 3 loser must be in the third "eighth" of the lower bracket.

The placement of the losers of subsequent rounds of play in the upper bracket is based on the relationship of second-round games to first-round games, third-round games to second-round games and to first-round games, and so forth. If upper bracket game 12 results from games 8 and 9, the loser of game 12 must be placed in a lower bracket position as far away as possible from the losers of games 8 and 9.

The objective of the adjustment of numbers is to delay for as long as possible the meeting of two entries for the second time in the tournament.

TOURNAMENT PROBLEM-SOLVING

This section involves calculations one can make to determine, in advance of drawing a bracket, the circumstances in which the tournament can be conducted. As was the case with single elimination, three variables require consideration in solving tournament problems: N, days, and games/day. By predetermining any two of the variables, one can solve for the third. All solutions to problems are based on the assumptions that no postponements are possible, and no entry plays more than once per day (or other time period).

Knowing N, the number of entries in the tournament, the following determinations can be made:

(1) The minimum number of games in the tournament = 2N -2

Example: N = 20

$$\text{minimum number of games} = 2N - 2$$
$$= 2 \times 20 - 2$$
$$= 38$$

(2) The maximum number of games in the tournament = 2N -1

Example: N = 20

$$\text{maximum number of games} = 2N - 1$$
$$= 2 \times 20 - 1$$
$$= 39$$

The difference between the minimum and maximum is one game. This is the extra game that must be played in the event that, in what could have been the final contest, the winner of the loser's bracket defeats the final survivor of the upper bracket. For scheduling purposes, it must be assumed that the extra game will be needed. The 2N - 1 formula is used for problem-solving.

A double elimination tournament for thirty-two entries is illustrated in Figure 2-6. The game numbers in the upper bracket are those without parentheses. The numbers without parentheses in the lower bracket represent the losers of the corresponding games in the upper bracket. The numbers in parentheses indicate days of play, and rounds of play, in reverse order. For example, an (8) means that the game for which it appears is played on the eighth to last day, and in the eighth to last round, of the tournament. A (1) indicates the last day, and round, of the tournament. Note that in order to denote days of play equal to rounds of play, the games available per day must be equal to the number of games in the largest round of the tournament.

The solutions to problems involving double elimination tournaments are best understood by working backward from the last game to the first round of the upper bracket. By working backward, the final rounds of a double elimination tournament can be standardized, just as those for single elimination tournaments are standardized. Single elimination brackets are drawn so that every round beyond the first round is a perfect round (i.e., a power of two), except the last round, which is only one game. Double elimination is more complicated, but the same concept can be applied.

A look at both the bracket (Fig. 2-6) and the chart (Fig. 2-7) shows that regardless of the number of games to be played per day, the last three games require one day each to play. Should two or more games per day be available, the last seven games can be played in five days. With four or more games available per day, the last fifteen games can be played in seven days. Eight or more games allow the last thirty-one games to be played in nine days. Sixteen or more games allow the last sixty-three games to be played in eleven days.

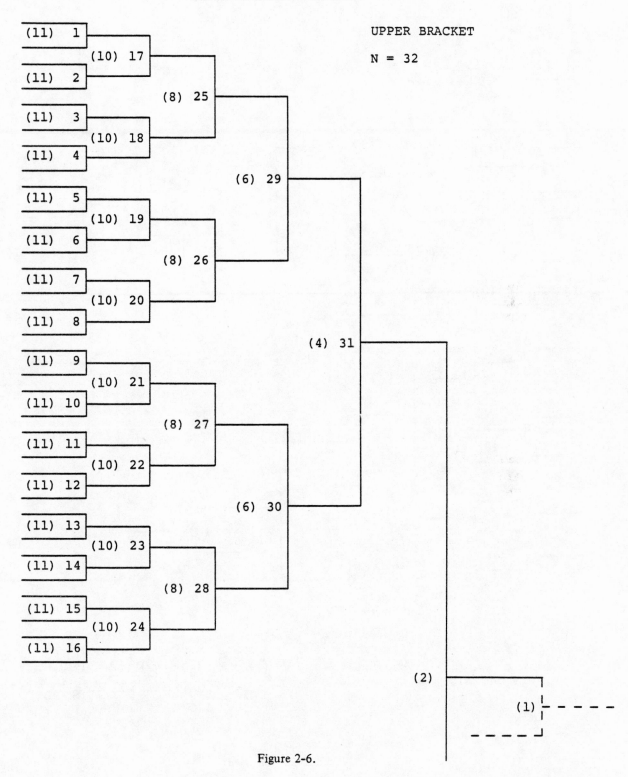

Figure 2-6.

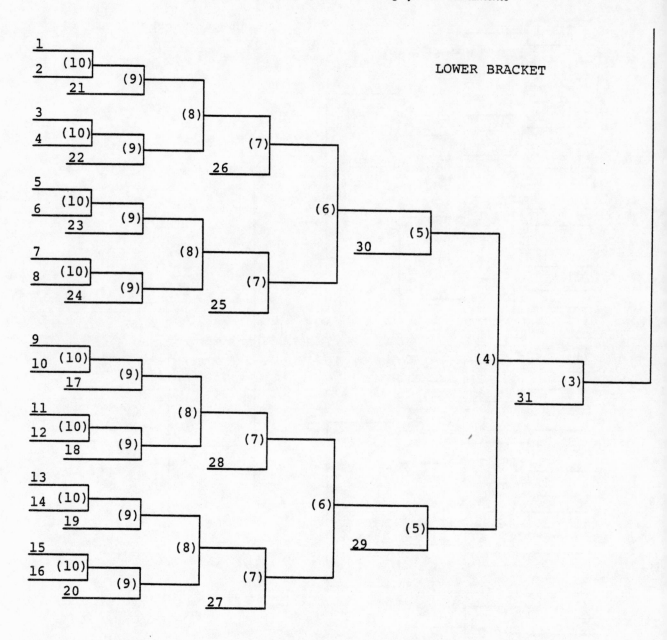

REMINDER: THE NUMBERS IN PARENTHESES,
           WHILE DENOTING DAYS OF PLAY
           IN REVERSE ORDER, ALSO
           INDICATE ROUNDS OF PLAY IN
           REVERSE ORDER.

Figure 2-6. (continued)

GAMES AVAILABLE PER DAY	NUMBER OF DAYS TO PLAY LAST NUMBER OF GAMES	MAXIMUM GAMES FOR EACH ROUND OF PLAY (rounds in reverse order)										
2 – 3	5 days for last 7 gms						2	2	1	1	1	
4 – 7	7 days for last 15 gms				4	4	2	2	1	1	1	
9 – 15	9 days for last 31 gms			8	8	4	4	2	2	1	1	1
16 – 31	11 days for last 63 gms	16	16	8	8	4	4	2	2	1	1	1

Figure 2-7.

Perfect rounds of play are established for double elimination tournaments of 4, 8, 16, and 32 entries. For example, the chart shows that a tournament for eight entries requires fifteen games and has seven rounds of play. A tournament for sixteen entries requires thirty-one games and has nine rounds of play.

From the chart, then, ratios can be set up and employed in establishing rounds of play and in solving tournament problems involving any number of entries. When establishing rounds of play, it must be noted that certain games in the upper bracket must be played before other games in the lower bracket. For instance, upper bracket games 25, 26, 27, and 28 must be played before those games in the lower bracket that involve the losers of the upper-bracket games. When working backward, therefore, the round in the loser's bracket, indicated by (7), is considered before the corresponding round in the upper bracket (8).

GAMES/DAY	RATIO
2 – 3	5 – 7
4 – 7	7 – 15
8 – 15	9 – 31
16 – 31	11 – 63

Rounds of play for tournaments that involve nonperfect rounds are established in the following manner.

Example: N = 14

Step 1: Determine the number of games in the tournament.

number of games = 2N - 1

$$= 2 \times 14 - 1$$

$$= 27$$

Step 2: Select the appropriate ratio — one whose number of games comes closest to the number of games in the tournament without exceeding that number.

Ratio: 7 - 15

Step 3: The ratio immediately establishes the final seven rounds of the tournament.

round	1	2	3	4	5	6	7
games	4	4	2	2	1	1	1

Step 4: Subtract those games (15) already accounted for from the total number of games in the tournament.

27 - 15 = 12 games remaining

Step 5: If the number of remaining games is equal to or less than the number of games in the last established round (seventh to last round in this case), establish the first round of the tournament with that number. If, however, the number of remaining games is greater than those in the last established round, the remaining games are divided by two and the first two rounds are established with those numbers.

remaining games = 12

games in the last established round = 4

Under the rule set forth above, the appropriate procedure in this case is to divide the number of remaining games (12) by two and establish the first two rounds.

12/2 = 6

The total sequence of rounds is:

round	1	2	3	4	5	6	7	8	9
games	6	6	4	4	2	2	1	1	1

Number of rounds = 9
Total games = 27

Example: N = 19

Step 1: number of games = 2N - 1

$$= 2 \times 19 - 1$$

$$= 37$$

Step 2: Appropriate ratio is 9 - 31

Step 3: The final nine rounds are established.

round	1	2	3	4	5	6	7	8	9
games	8	8	4	4	2	2	1	1	1

Step 4: 37 - 31 = 6 games remaining

Step 5: Six games is less than those (8) in the last established round. Therefore, the first round consists of six games, and the total sequence of rounds is as follows:

round	1	2	3	4	5	6	7	8	9	10
games	6	8	8	4	4	2	2	1	1	1

Number of rounds = 10
Total games = 37

Problem Type I

Knowing the number of entries and the number of games that can be played each day, determine the minimum number of days required to run the tournament.

Example 1

Known: N = 13 and games/day = 4

Step 1: Determine the number of games in the tournament.

$$\text{number of games} = 2N - 1$$

$$= 2 \times 13 - 1$$

$$= 25$$

Step 2: Determine the largest round of the tournament. The largest round of a double elimination tournament is determined as either the first or second round of the upper bracket. Since the upper bracket is a simple single elimination draw, the numbers of first- and second-round games are found as follows:

first-round games = N - next lower power of two

$$= 13 - 8$$

$$= 5$$

second-round games = next lower power of two divided by 2

$$= 8/2$$

$$= 4$$

The largest round of the tournament, therefore, is the first round, which has five games. Since the number of games played per day cannot exceed the largest round of the tournament, the games per day must be less than or equal to the number of games in the largest round. Should a situation arise in which the number of games available per day exceeds the largest round, simply reduce the games per day to equal the number of games in the largest round.

games/day = 4

largest round = 5

no adjustment necessary

Step 3: Establish a ratio that corresponds to the games played per day, and subtract the number of games in that ratio from the number of games in the tournament to find the games remaining. With four games per day, the appropriate ratio is 7 - 15.

$$\begin{array}{r} 25 \\ 7 - 15 \\ \hline 10 \text{ games remaining} \end{array}$$

Step 4: Find the days needed to play the remaining number of games by dividing the remaining games by the games played per day. Always round off to higher number.

10/4 = 3 days

Step 5: Add the number of days used in the ratio and the days found in Step 4 to arrive at the number of days needed to run the tournament.

number of days = 7 + 3

$$= 10$$

Answer: 10 days

Example 2

Known: N = 13 and 9 games/day

Step 1: Number of games ∵ 2N - 1

$$= 2 \times 13 - 1$$

$$= 25$$

Step 2: first-round games = 13 - 8

$$= 5$$

second-round games = 8/2

$$= 4$$

largest round = 5

games/day = 9

The number of games that can be played per day must be reduced from nine to five.

Step 3:   25

7 - 15

10 games remain

Step 4: 10/5 = 2 days

Step 5: 7 + 2 = 9

Answer: nine days

Example 3

Known: N = 23 and x games/day, where x represents the minimum number of games per day that must be available in order to run the tournament in a minimum number of days.

Step 1: number of games = 2N - 1

$$= 2 \times 23 - 1$$

$$= 45$$

Step 2: first-round games = 23 - 16

$$= 7$$

second-round games = 16/2

$$= 8$$

The largest round is eight, so eight games must be available per day.

Step 3:   45

    9 - $\underline{31}$

       14 games remain

Step 4:   14/8 = 2 days

Step 5:   9 + 2 = 11

Answer: eleven days

Note: The solution to the above problem can also be used to determine the number of rounds in the tournament.

Example 4

Known: N = 10, 19, 36 and 7 games/day. The three tournaments are to be run simultaneously.

Step 1:   Determine the number of games for each tournament.

       number of games = 2N - 1

$$= 2 \times 10 - 1$$

$$= 19$$

       number of games = 2N - 1

$$= 2 \times 19 - 1$$

$$= 37$$

       number of games = 2N - 1

$$= 2 \times 36 - 1$$

$$= 71$$

Step 2:   Set up the number of rounds and games for each round of each tournament. Add vertically to get the total number of games for each round.

round	1	2	3	4	5	6	7	8	9	10	11	12
games (N = 10)					4	4	4	2	2	1	1	1
games (N = 19)			6	8	8	4	4	2	2	1	1	1
games (N = 36)	8	16	16	8	8	4	4	2	2	1	1	1
total games	8	16	22	16	20	12	12	6	6	3	3	3

Step 3: With seven games available for play each day, eliminate as many final rounds as possible.

round	1	2	3	4	5	6	7	8	9	10	11	12
total games	8	16	22	16	20	12	12	6	6	3	3	3
days								1	1	1	1	1

Step 4: Start with the first round and eliminate the remaining rounds. Note: Because of the complicated nature of double elimination play, special care must be taken to avoid scheduling entries for play more than once per day. Particular problems occur in this regard when large numbers of games can be played per day. Large numbers often allow the scheduling of an invalid number of games per day. In the interests of caution and speed of calculation, therefore, it is suggested that games be scheduled conservatively. When complications and doubt arise during the process of calculating numbers of days to complete rounds of play, days should be assigned liberally to "play it safe." This procedure may or may not result in the absolute minimum number of days required to run the tournaments, but a quick, relatively accurate estimation is achieved. Further, the established estimate is always one where, in actual scheduling, no additional days are ever required to run the tournaments. To the contrary, one or two less than estimated may be sufficient.

round	1	2	3	4	5	6	7	8	9	10	11	12
total games	8	16	22	16	20	12	12	6	6	1	1	1
		-6	-4	-3	-1	-2	-4					
		10	18	13	19	10	8					
days	2	2	3	2	3	2	2	1	1	1	1	1

Answer: twenty-one days

Problem Type II

Knowing the number of entries and the number of days available to run the tournament, determine the minimum number of games per day required to run the tournament.

Example 1

Known: N = 12 and 10 days

Step 1:   Determine the number of games in the tournament.

$$\text{number of games} = 2N - 1$$
$$= 2 \times 12 - 1$$
$$= 23$$

Step 2:   Divide the number of games by the number of days available. This results in an index number which, in turn, indicates the appropriate ratio. Index numbers are considered as games per day when related to ratios: an index of three would result in a 5 - 7 ratio, and an index of 6 a 7 - 15 ratio. Always round off to the higher number.

$$23/10 = 3$$

5 - 7 ratio is appropriate

Step 3:   Subtract the number of final games in the ratio from the games in the tournament.

$$\begin{array}{r} 23 \\ 5 - \underline{7} \\ \text{16 games remain} \end{array}$$

Step 4:   Five days have been used to play the last seven games. Divide the remaining number of days (5) into the remaining number of games (16) to find the required number of games that must be available per day. Always round off to the higher number.

$$16/5 = 4$$

Four is the correct answer as long as it does not exceed the number of games in the largest round. The largest round of the tournament is four.

Answer: four games/day

Example 2

Known: N = 8 and 6 days

Step 1:   number of games = 2N - 1

$$= 2 \times 8 - 1$$
$$= 15$$

Step 2:   15/6 = 3 (index number)

Step 3:   15
      5 - 7
      ——
         8 games remaining
         1 day remaining

Step 4: 8/1 = 8 games/day

The answer is incorrect because eight is greater than the largest round of the tournament (4). The tournament is impossible to run in six days. This conclusion could have been reached immediately by noting that it takes at least seven days to play the last fifteen games. If seven days were available, then:

Step 2a: 15/7 = 3 (index number)

Step 3a: 15
       5 - 7
       ——
          8 games remaining
          2 days remaining

Step 4a: 8/2 = 4
Answer: four games per day

Problem Type III

Knowing the number of days available to run the tournament and the number of games that can be played each day, determine the maximum number of entries that can be accommodated in the tournament.

Example 1

Known: 10 days and 4 games/day

Step 1: The number of games per day (4) leads to a ratio of 7 - 15.

Step 2: Seven days have been used to play 15 games. Determine the remaining days, and multiply them times the available games per day (4) to find the number of possible remaining games.

      10 - 7 = 3 days remaining

      3 x 4 = 12 games remaining

Step 3: Add the number of remaining games (12) to the number of games in the ratio (15) to find the number of games in the tournament.

      12 + 15 = 27 games

Step 4: Inject the number of games (27) into the formula to find N.

$$2N - 1 = 27$$
$$2N = 28$$
$$N = 14$$

Step 5: Before accepting the answer as correct, determine the largest round in the tournament and check it against the games per day. If the games per day is greater than the largest round, the answer is incorrect.

games per day = 4
largest round = 6

Answer: fourteen entries

Example 2

Known: 10 days and 3 games/day

Step 1: Three games per day leads to a ratio of 5 - 7.

Step 2: 10 - 5 = 5 days remaining
5 x 3 = 15 games remaining

Step 3: 7 + 15 = 22 games in the tournament

Step 4: $2N - 1 = 22$

$$2N = 23$$

$N = 11\frac{1}{2}$ (round off to lower number)

$$N = 11$$

Step 5: games/day = 3
largest round = 4

Answer: eleven entries

Example 3

Known: 8 days and 7 games/day

Step 1: Seven games per day leads to a ratio of 7 - 15.

Step 2: 8 - 7 = 1 day remaining
1 x 7 = 7 games remaining

Step 3: 7 + 15 = 22 games in the tournament

Step 4:   2N - 1 = 22

$$2N = 23$$

$$N = 11\tfrac{1}{2}$$

$$N = 11$$

Step 5:   games per day = 7
            largest round = 4

Answer is invalid and the tournament cannot be run under the given circumstances. The number of games per day must be reduced, or the number of days must be increased, until the correct answer is found. Try five games per day.

Step 1a: Five games per day leads to a ratio of 7 - 15.

Step 2a: 8 - 7 = 1 day remaining

$$1 \times 5 = 5 \text{ remaining games}$$

Step 3a: 15 + 5 = 20 games in the tournament

Step 4a: 2 N - 1 = 20

$$2N = 21$$

$$N = 10\tfrac{1}{2}$$

$$N = 10$$

Step 5a: games per day = 5
            largest round = 4

Answer is still incorrect. Try four games per day.

Step 1b: Four games per day leads to a ratio of 7 - 15.

Step 2b: 8 - 7 = 1 day remaining
            1 x 4 = 4 games remaining

Step 3b: 4 + 15 = 19 games in the tournament

Step 4b: 2N - 1 = 19

$$2N = 20$$

$$N = 10$$

Step 5b: games per day = 4
            largest round = 4
Answer: ten entries

Chapter III
TRIPLE ELIMINATION TOURNAMENT

THIS tournament goes one step beyond double elimination by stipulating that the winner of the tournament is the entry that remains after all other entries lose three contests. A draw for ten entries appears in Figure 3-1.

Note that the tournament bracket can be seen as three individual single elimination brackets. A loss in the top bracket results in a placement in the middle bracket, and a loss in the middle bracket leads to a drop to the lower bracket. After entry into the final bracket, a subsequent loss eliminates an entry from the tournament.

The numbers in the upper bracket indicate games of play, in sequence. Parenthesized numbers in the middle bracket also represent games of play. Nonparenthesized numbers represent the losers of the corresponding games in the upper bracket. The lower bracket contains numbers that represent the losers of the corresponding games in the middle bracket. Other notations are explained in subsequent paragraphs.

All triple elimination tournaments proceed in the same way until a certain point is reached. That point is at game (9), at which time two situations can occur. Both are explained in the following contingencies.

Contingency 1

Entry A defeats entry B in game (9) and advances to line Q with no losses. Game (10) is unnecessary and entry B, with two losses, drops to the appropriate slot in the lower bracket. Then, the winner of game R (lower bracket) plays entry A in game I. If entry A wins that game, the tournament is over because all but one entry have three losses. To win the tournament, the survivor of the lower bracket must defeat entry A three times in a row.

56

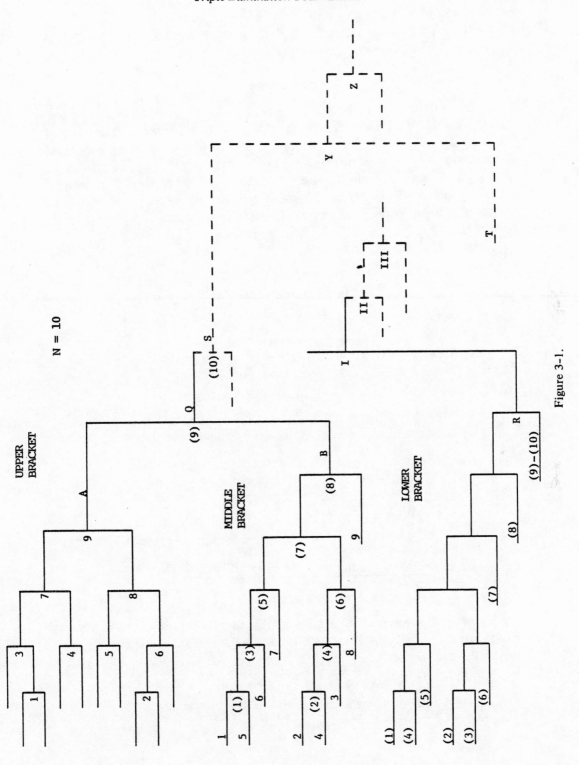

Figure 3-1.

Game II would be necessary only if entry A lost game I. By the same token, game III would be necessary only if entry A lost a second time. The tournament winner would then be determined by game III.

Contingency 2

Entry B defeats entry A, which results in each entry having one loss and makes game (10) necessary. The winner of game (10) advances to line S, and the loser drops to the appropriate line in the lower bracket. The winner of game R (lower bracket) proceeds to line T with two losses. The entries on lines S and T play in game Y. The tournament is over if game Y is won by the entry on line S. Otherwise, game Z would be necessary and would be contended for by entries that have two losses. The winner of game Z is the tournament champion.

Given N, the number of entries in the tournament, the following determinations can be made:

$$\text{number of games in tournament} = 3N - 1$$

Example: N = 10

$$\text{number of games} = 3N - 1$$
$$= 3 \times 10 - 1$$
$$= 29$$

As with double elimination, ratios can be determined to aid in problem solving. The assumption is made that no entry plays more than once per day.

Games/Day	Number of Days to Play Last Number of Games
2 - 3	8 days for last 11 games
4 - 7	11 days for last 23 games
8 - 15	14 days for last 47 games

Problem Type I

Knowing the number of entries in the tournament and the number of games that can be played per day, determine the number of days required to run the tournament.

Known: N = 10 and 4 games/day

Step 1: Determine the number of games in the tournament.

$$\text{number of games} = 3N - 1$$
$$= 3 \times 10 - 1$$
$$= 29$$

Step 2: Determine the largest round of the tournament. The largest round of a triple elimination tournament is either the first or second round of the upper bracket.

largest round = 4

games per day = 4

no adjustment necessary

Step 3: Establish a ratio that corresponds to the games played per day, and subtract the number of games in that ratio from the number of games in the tournament to find the games remaining. With four games per day, the appropriate ratio is 11 - 23.

$$\begin{array}{r} 29 \\ 11 - \underline{23} \\ \hline 6 \text{ games remaining} \end{array}$$

Step 4: Find the days needed to play the remaining number of games by dividing the remaining games by the games played per day.

6/4 = 2 days

Step 5: Add the number of days used in the ratio and the days found in step (4) to arrive at the number of days needed to run the tournament.

number of days = 11 + 2

= 13

Answer: thirteen days

Chapter IV
CONTINUAL RANDOMIZATION
ELIMINATION TOURNAMENT

THIS tournament design is very similar to those for single elimination, double elimination, and consolation tournaments. The flow of continual randomization differs, however, in these respects: (1) There is no tournament bracket. Rather, a line sheet is used to list entries (see Fig. 4-1). (2) Entries are taken just before play begins. (3) For each round of play, entries are matched against each other by random draw. (4) There is the possibility of having one bye in any of the rounds, except the last.

The use of this structure is mostly geared to the short-term intramural tournament. For certain sports, it can also be used for tournaments that span several days, or for tournaments held in physical education classes. For the short-term intramural tournament, where entries would be expected to play several contests within the course of a day, the activity (table tennis, for example) would have to be of a sufficiently nonstrenuous nature so undue fatigue does not affect play. Also, the contests, themselves, should be of a rather short duration (15 minutes, perhaps), so each round of play can be completed in a reasonable time.

The differences in structure and procedure of continual randomization, from the standard elimination tournaments, virtually eliminate the possibility of forfeits and, therefore, substantially improve the prospect of actual play for those people who appear for a tournament.

To demonstrate the structure and flow of continual randomization, for a single elimination situation, the procedures for an individual sport competition are described below. It is assumed that the factors (number of entries, number of play areas, etc.) contributing to the length of the tournament allow for its completion in a short time.

ROUND 1 NAME	NUMBER	OPPONENT NUMBER	MATCH NUMBER	bEING PLAYED	WINNERS AND SCORES
JARVIS	1				
HANEY	2	12	1	X	
SPINO	3				
HARVEY	4				
HANLY	5				
REIKER	6	9	4	X	
HOLLIS	7				
BARRIS	8	16	3	X	
ZINK	9	6	4	X	
MALO	10				
PARIS	11				
OTT	12	2	1	X	
TABOR	13	–	–	–	
CASTLE	14				
ANCEL	15				
GANT	16	8	3	X	
PARKS	17				
ROSS	18				
TALLY	19	21	2	X	
NABOR	20				
ISSEL	21	19	2	X	

Figure 4-1.

SINGLE ELIMINATION

No entries are taken before the actual day of the tournament. Contestants enter within a half-hour period directly before play is to begin. As players check in with the tournament supervisor, their names are listed on a line sheet (Fig.4-1). Numbers are assigned to the names in order of their entry on the sheet. After all entries are in, a group of numbered cards is deposited in a box for purposes of random draw. Each entry is represented by one of the numbered cards.

Matches are determined by the random selection of numbers out of the box. The first two numbers form the first match, the second two numbers form the second match, and so forth. Each match is recorded twice on the line sheet by pairing each player's number with his/her opponent's number (Fig. 4-1). Match numbers are assigned in the order that they are formed from the draw, and matches are played in that order. The first sequence of matches on the four play areas available in Figure 4-1 are Haney versus Ott, Reiker versus Zink, Barris versus Gant, and Tally versus Issel. Note that matches are checked as "being played," as players are assigned to play areas. In this particular example, Tabor (number 13) was the only player whose card was not chosen, so he/she gets a bye for the first round. His/her name is immediately transferred to the line sheet for the second round. (Fig. 4-3).

The match scores are recorded only after the names of the winners. Figure 4-2 illustrates the completed first round. Winners are immediately transferred to the line sheet for the next round, and they are assigned numbers.

ROUND 1 NAME	NUMBER	OPPONENT NUMBER	MATCH NUMBER	BEING PLAYED	WINNERS AND SCORES
JARVIS	1	17	9	X	21-5,21-7
HANEY	2	12	1	X	
SPINO	3	5	8	X	
HARVEY	4	15	7	X	21-19,21-10
HANLY	5	3	8	X	21-11,21-16
REIKER	6	9	4	X	
HOLLIS	7	20	10	X	21-7,21-11
BARRIS	8	16	3	X	21-3,21-5
ZINK	9	6	4	X	21-13,21-14
MALO	10	11	5	X	
PARIS	11	10	5	X	21-8,21-18
OTT	12	2	1	X	21-5,21-7
TABOR	13	-	-	-	------
CASTLE	14	18	6	X	
ANCEL	15	4	7	X	
GANT	16	8	3	X	
PARKS	17	1	9	X	
ROSS	18	14	6	X	21-17,21-9
TALLY	19	21	2	X	21-2,21-5
NABOR	20	7	10	X	
ISSEL	21	19	2	X	

Figure 4-2.

In round 2 (Fig. 4-3), eleven participants are listed. If there is a significant time lapse (several hours, for instance) between the playing of rounds, a roll call of remaining contestants should be made before the draw for matches. Should someone not be present for the start of a round, he/she is eliminated from the tournament before he/she is scheduled for a match. Thus, a forfeit is averted. When it is determined that all eleven players are actually present to play the second round, eleven numbered cards are placed in the box, and matches are again formed by a random draw. Ott receives a bye and is placed in the third round. If it had happened that the number of Tabor (first-round bye) again remained in the box after all other numbers were selected, he/she would be matched with the player whose number was selected second-to-last. The player whose number was last selected would then be given the bye. Through that procedure, no player may receive more than one bye per tournament. The same system is applied to the formation and playing of the remaining rounds (Figures 4-4, 4-5, 4-6). Ott is the winner of the tournament.

ROUND 2 NAME	NUMBER	OPPONENT NUMBER	MATCH NUMBER	BEING PLAYED	WINNERS AND SCORES
TABOR	1	6	2	X	21-4,21-10
JARVIS	2	10	5	X	
HARVEY	3	7	4	X	21-17,21-15
HANLY	4	11	1	X	
HOLLIS	5	8	3	X	21-5,9-21,21-1
BARRIS	6	1	2	X	
ZINK	7	3	4	X	
PARIS	8	5	3	X	
OTT	9	–	–	–	-----
ROSS	10	2	5	X	21-9, 21-3
TALLY	11	4	1	X	21-5,21-4

Figure 4-3.

ROUND 3 NAME	NUMBER	OPPONENT NUMBER	MATCH NUMBER	BEING PLAYED	WINNERS AND SCORES
OTT	1	3	1	X	21-9, 21-8
TABOR	2	4	3	X	
HOLLIS	3	1	1	X	
HARVEY	4	2	3	X	21-4, 21-9
TALLY	5	6	2	X	21-10, 21-4
ROSS	6	5	2	X	

Figure 4- 4.

ROUND 4 NAME	NUMBER	OPPONENT NUMBER	MATCH NUMBER	BEING PLAYED	WINNERS AND SCORES
OTT	1	3	1	X	21-13, 21-10
TALLY	2	-	-	-	-----
HARVEY	3	1	1	X	

Figure 4-5.

ROUND 5 NAME	NUMBER	OPPONENT NUMBER	MATCH NUMBER	BEING PLAYED	WINNERS AND SCORES
TALLY	1	2	1	X	
OTT	2	1	1	X	21-6, 21-6

Figure 4-6.

Double Elimination

The procedures for double elimination situations are exactly the same as for single elimination, except that provisions must be made for the meeting of those players who have one loss. After the first round of play, succeeding rounds (except the last two or three) must involve two line sheets — one for those players who have yet to lose, and one for those players with one loss.

To demonstrate the procedure, it will be assumed that the circumstances already presented in Figures 4-2 through 4-6 represent the round by round play among those players who have yet to lose. In round 1, ten players lost, so they are placed on a line sheet designated as round 1a (Fig. 4-7). The process for developing matches is the same as previously described. The winners move on to the line sheet for round 2a (Fig. 4-8), and the losers are eliminated from further competition. The players involved in round 2a matches include the winners of round 1a and the losers of round 2 (Fig.4-3). Round 3a involves the losers from round 3 and the winners from round 2a.

ROUND 1a NAME	NUMBER	OPPONENT NUMBER	MATCH NUMBER	BEING PLAYED	WINNERS AND SCORES
HANEY	1	4	5	X	5 - 3
SPINO	2	5	2	X	
REIKER	3	7	1	X	4 - 3
MALO	4	1	5	X	
CASTLE	5	2	2	X	1 - 0
ANCEL	6	10	4	X	
GANT	7	3	1	X	
PARKS	8	9	3	X	
NABOR	9	8	3	X	2 - 1
ISSEL	10	6	4	X	4 - 0

Figure 4-7.

ROUND 2a / NAME	NUMBER	OPPONENT NUMBER	MATCH NUMBER	BEING PLAYED	WINNERS AND SCORES
HANEY	1				
REIKER	2				
CASTLE	3				
NABOR	4				
ISSEL	5				
JARVIS	6				
HANLY	7				
BARRIS	8				
ZINK	9				
PARIS	10				

Figure 4-8.

The process is continued until only one player remains in each of the two lines of play. The two survivors (one without a loss, and one with one loss) are matched against each other in what could be the final contest. The extra match is made, if necessary.

Chapter V
TYPE I CONSOLATION TOURNAMENT

BRACKET CONSTRUCTION

T HE tournament consists of one single elimination championship bracket and one single elimination consolation bracket. Only first-game losers are placed in the consolation bracket. No entry in the consolation bracket has a chance at the regular championship, but a consolation champion is determined. The intent of the consolation tournament is to guarantee each entry the playing of at least two contests, without playing as many games as a double elimination tournament.

The rules of a single elimination draw apply to the construction of both championship and consolation brackets. An example for eight entries is illustrated in Figure 5-1. First, a single elimination bracket is drawn for eight entries. Then, the number of all possible first-game losers (four, in this case) is determined, and a single elimination bracket is drawn for that number.

CHAMPIONSHIP BRACKET

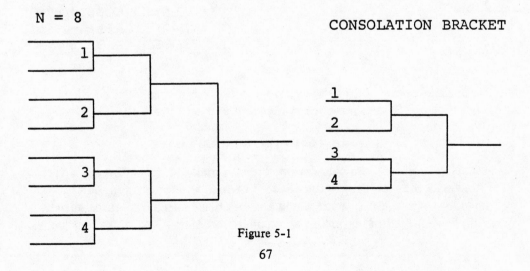

N = 8

CONSOLATION BRACKET

Figure 5-1

67

When byes are involved in the championship bracket, it is impossible to determine accurately the exact number of first-game losers. An example for ten entries appears in Figure 5-2. At least four first-game losers can be immediately identified as coming from games 1, 2, 4, and 5 of the championship bracket. However, two more first-game losers might arise from games 3 and 6. Should the entries that had byes lose, the total number of first-game losers would be six. The consolation bracket must, therefore, provide for the maximum possibility of six.

CHAMPIONSHIP BRACKET

N = 10

CONSOLATION BRACKET

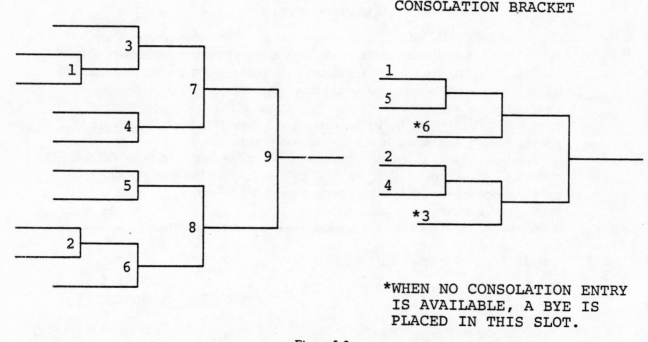

*WHEN NO CONSOLATION ENTRY IS AVAILABLE, A BYE IS PLACED IN THIS SLOT.

Figure 5-2.

For ease of scheduling, byes in the consolation bracket are assigned to entries that had first-round byes in the championship bracket.

TOURNAMENT PROBLEM SOLVING

This section involves calculations one can make to determine, in advance of drawing a bracket, the circumstances in which the tournament can be conducted. As was the case with single and double elimination, three variables require consideration in solving tournament problems: N, days, and games per day. Since Type I Consolation is infrequently employed, only one type of problem solution is demonstrated. By predetermining N and games per day, the number of days required to conduct the tournament can be established. The solution is based on the assumption that no postponements are possible, and no entry plays more than once per day (or other time period). Several considerations require preliminary attention.

The number of second-round games in a single elimination tournament is determined as follows:

$$N = 23$$

Step 1: Determine the next lower power of two.

$$NLPT = 16$$

Step 2: Divide NLPT by two.

$$16/2 = 8 \text{ second-round games}$$

Since the number of first-game losers cannot be accurately identified, the number of games in the tournament also cannot be determined; however, the maximum number of games can be found. There are two formulas — one for each of two situations.

When the number of first-round games of the championship bracket exceeds the number of second-round games (as it does for N = 13), the maximum number of first-game losers is determined by adding the number of first-round games to the number of byes in the championship bracket.

Step 1: Determine the number of first and second-round games.

$$\text{first-round games} = N - NLPT$$
$$= 13 - 8$$
$$= 5$$
$$\text{second-round games} = NLPT/2$$
$$= 8/2$$
$$= 4$$

Step 2: Determine the number of byes in the championship bracket.

$$\text{byes} = NHPT - N$$
$$= 16 - 13$$
$$= 3$$

Step 3: Determine the maximum number of first-game losers.

$$\text{losers} = \text{1st-rd. games} + \text{byes}$$
$$= 5 + 3$$
$$= 8$$

The maximum number of games in the tournament is found by adding the numbers of games in the championship and consolation brackets.

Step 1:   consolation bracket

$$\text{max. games} = N - 1$$
$$= 8 - 1$$
$$= 7$$

Step 2:   championship bracket

$$\text{max. games} = N - 1$$
$$= 13 - 1$$
$$= 12$$

Step 3:   tournament

$$\text{max. games} = \text{championship} + \text{consolation}$$
$$= 12 + 7$$
$$= 19$$

The above-described method is actually the long way of arriving at the answer to the problem. For the quickest solution, follow these steps:

Step 1:   Determine the numbers of first and second-round games.

Step 2a: If the number of first-round games is greater than that for second-round games, use this formula:

max. tournament games = N + lst- rd. gms. + byes - 2

Step 2b: If the number of first-round games is less than or equal to the number of second-round games, use this formula:

max. tournament games = N + lst-rd. gms. + 2nd-rd. gms. - 2

As in double elimination, the solutions to Type I Consolation problems are best understood by working backward from the final to the first round.

The chart in Figure 5-3 describes the relationships between available games per day, ratios, and rounds of play.

GAMES AVAILABLE PER DAY	NUMBER OF DAYS TO PLAY LAST NUMBER OF GAMES	MAXIMUM GAMES FOR EACH ROUND OF PLAY (ROUNDS IN REVERSE ORDER)			
		4	3	2	1
2 – 3	1 day for last 2 gms (1-2)				2
4 – 7	2 days for last 6 gms (2-6)			4	2
8 – 15	3 days for last 14 gms (3-14)		8	4	2
16 – 31	4 days for last 30 gms (4-30)	16	8	4	2

Figure 5-3.

Rounds of play are established in the following manner.

$$N = 13$$

Step 1: Determine the number of games and the largest round in the tournament.

> number of games = 19
> largest round   = 5

Step 2: Use the number of games in the largest round as the games available per day. Determine the appropriate ratio and set up rounds of play to that point.

With five games per day, the appropriate ratio is: 2 - 6

round	2	1
games	4	2

Step 3: Determine the number of remaining rounds required to complete the tournament. Subtract the number of games in the ratio from the tournament games to find the remaining games. Divide the remaining games by the available games per day.

> 19 - 6 = 13 games remaining
> 13/5 = 3 rounds remaining

Step 4: When three rounds remain, the first round of the tournament is the first round of the championship bracket. The second round is the second round of the championship bracket; the third round consists of the games that remain.

round	1	2	3	4	5
games	5	4	4	4	2

Note: When only two rounds remain, divide the remaining games by two and insert the games appropriately in the first two rounds.

Problem Type I

Knowing the number of entries and the number of games that can be played per day, determine the minimum number of days required to run the tournament.

Example 1

Known: N = 15 and 5 games/day

Step 1: Determine the number of games in the tournament.

$$\text{max. games} = N + \text{1st rd. gms.} + \text{byes} - 2$$
$$= 15 + 7 + 1 - 2$$
$$= 21$$

Step 2: Determine the largest round of the tournament and compare it to the number of available games per day. Where appropriate, games per day must be reduced to equal the largest round of the tournament. The largest round of the tournament is determined as either the first or second round of the championship bracket.

games/day = 5
largest round = 7
no adjustment necessary

Step 3: Select the appropriate ratio and subtract the number of games in the ratio from the number of games in the tournament to find the remaining games.

With five games per day, use the 2 - 6 ratio (2 days for last 6 games).

$$\begin{array}{r} 21 \\ 2 - 6 \\ \hline 15 \text{ games remaining} \end{array}$$

Step 4: Divide the remaining number of games by the games played per day to find the number of days required to play the remaining games.

15/5 = 3 days

Step 5: Add the number of days used in the ratio and the days found in step (4) to arrive at the number of days needed to run the tournament.

2 + 3 = 5

Answer: five days

Example 2

Known: N = 16 and 9 games/day

Step 1:   max. games = N + 1st rd. gms.. - 2

$$= 16 + 8 - 2$$

$$= 22$$

Step 2:   games/day = 9
largest round = 8
must reduce to 8 games/day

Step 3:   Appropriate ratio is 3 - 14.

$$\begin{array}{r} 22 \\ 3 - \underline{14} \\ \hline 8 \text{ games remaining} \end{array}$$

Step 4:   8/8 = 1 day

Step 5:   3 + 1 = 4
Answer: four days

Chapter VI
TYPE II CONSOLATION TOURNAMENT

BRACKET CONSTRUCTION

TYPE II consolation is very similar to a double elimination tournament. It consists, however, of two unconnected brackets. The championship bracket is a single elimination draw. The winner of the final game is the tournament champion, while the loser is the second-place finisher. All losers, except the loser of the final game of the championship bracket, are eventually placed in the consolation bracket. Placement is made in exactly the same way as double elimination. The winner of the consolation bracket is the third-place finisher. No entry that loses a game has a chance at the championship.

A tournament for eighteen entries is shown in Figure 6-1. The consolation draw is similar to that for double elimination, except that the last three games of a double elimination tournament are omitted.

TOURNAMENT PROBLEM-SOLVING

With only two differences, tournament problems are solved in the same manner as those for double elimination. The number of games in a Type II Consolation tournament is found through using the formula: 2N - 4.

Example: N = 10

$$games = 2N - 4$$
$$= 2 \times 10 - 4$$
$$= 16$$

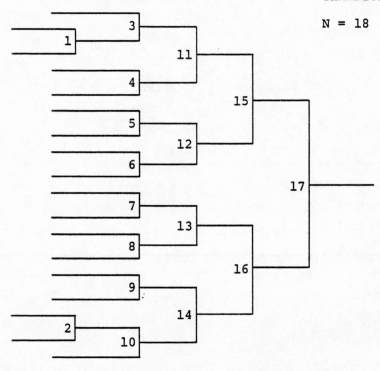

CHAMPIONSHIP BRACKET

N = 18

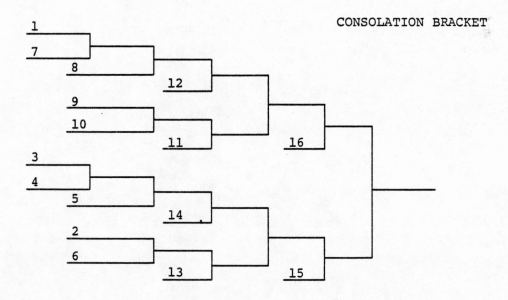

CONSOLATION BRACKET

Figure 6-1.

The other difference is reflected in the chart below, which describes the relationships between available games per day, ratios, and rounds of play. For details on solutions to tournament problems, refer to the chapter on double elimination tournaments.

Games Available Per Day	Number of Days to Play Last Number of Games	Maximum Games for Each Round of Play (Rounds in Reverse Order)							
		8	7	6	5	4	3	2	1
2 - 3	2 days for last 4 gms (2 - 4)							2	2
4 - 7	4 days for last 12 gms (4 - 12)					4	4	2	2
8 - 15	6 days for last 28 gms (6 - 28)			8	8	4	4	2	2
16 - 31	8 days for last 60 gms (8 - 60)	16	16	8	8	4	4	2	2

Chapter VII
BAGNALL-WILD CONSOLATION TOURNAMENT

T HE purpose of this tournament is to determine realistic second and third-place finishers. As illustrated in Figure 7-1, it consists of a championship bracket and at least one, possibly two, consolation brackets. Although the consolation rounds of Bagnall-Wild are of more significance than those of other tournaments, entries must wait for the determination of a champion before they know whether or not they play again. There is no guarantee that each entry plays more than once. Because of the cumbersome nature of this tournament, and the limited possibilities for its use, tournament problem-solving is not discussed.

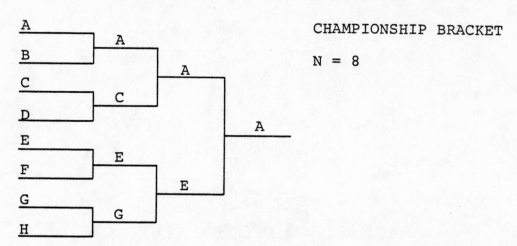

CHAMPIONSHIP BRACKET

N = 8

THOSE ENTRIES DEFEATED
BY THE CHAMPION COMPETE
FOR SECOND AND THIRD PLACES.

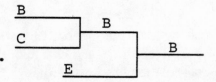

2nd PLACE: B   3rd PLACE: E

BUT, IF THE
FOLLOWING OCCURS,

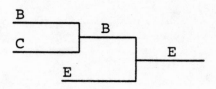

2nd PLACE: E

THOSE TEAMS WHICH WERE
DEFEATED BY E COMPETE
FOR THIRD PLACE.

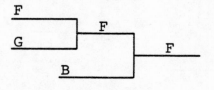

3rd PLACE: F

Figure 7-1.

In drawing the brackets, the maximum possibility must always be provided, so the tournament is drawn with two consolation brackets. A tournament draw for twelve entries is shown in Figure 7-2. Whenever circumstances allow, the loser in the final round of the championship bracket is given a bye in the consolation bracket.

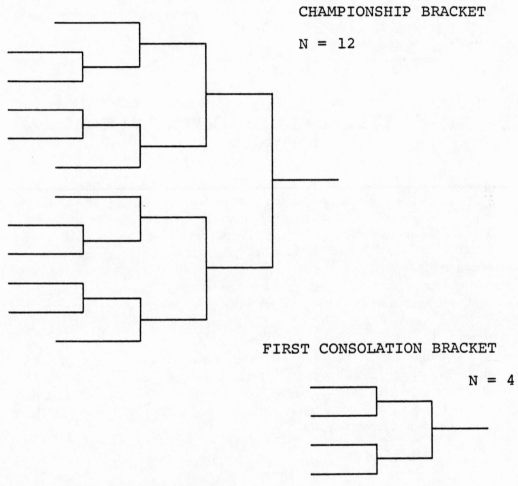

CHAMPIONSHIP BRACKET

N = 12

FIRST CONSOLATION BRACKET

N = 4

SECOND CONSOLATION BRACKET

N = 5

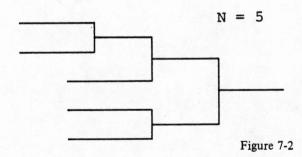

Figure 7-2

Chapter VIII
MUELLER-ANDERSON PLAYBACK
TOURNAMENT

THE concept of the tournament was developed by Pat Mueller and Bruce Anderson, both of the University of Minnesota, and its purpose is to determine a place ranking for all entries. The tournament consists of a single elimination championship bracket and a number of consolation brackets. An example for eleven entries is illustrated in Figure 8-1.

Each round of play results in a number of losers. The loser of the final game (10) automatically receives second place, but all other losers must play the losers within their respective rounds of play to determine place finishes. The losers of games 8 and 9 play for third place, with the loser of that game getting fourth place. The four losers in round two vie for fifth, sixth, seventh, and eighth places. The winner of game (3) gets fifth and the loser receives sixth place. The losers of games (1) and (2) play for seventh and eighth places. Similarly, the three losers in the first round play for ninth, tenth, and eleventh places.

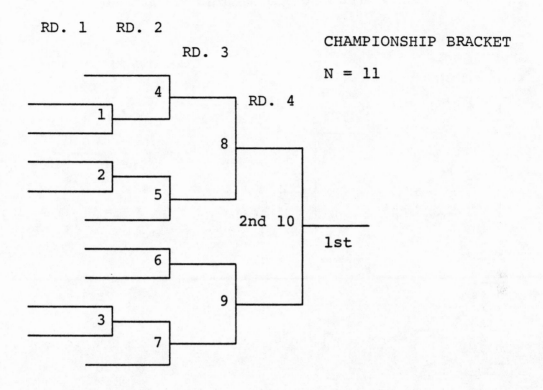

CHAMPIONSHIP BRACKET

N = 11

ROUND 1 PLAYOFF

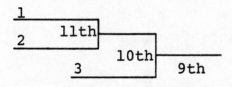

ROUND 2 PLAYOFF

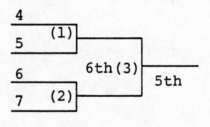

ROUND 3 PLAYOFF

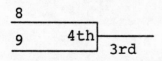

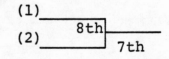

Figure 8-1.

Figure 8-2 shows another example, this time for twenty-one entries.

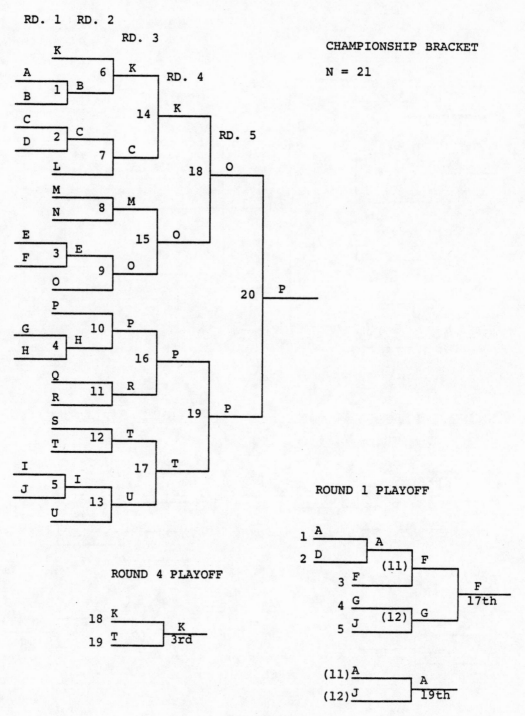

Figure 8-2.

ROUND 2 PLAYOFF

ROUND 3 PLAYOFF

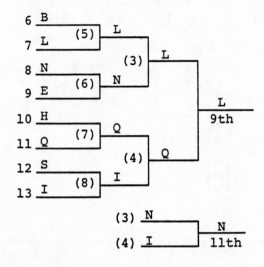

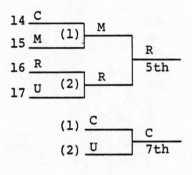

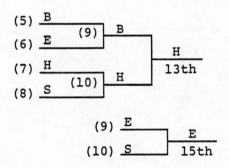

RANKING

1st	P
2nd	O
3rd	K
4th	T
5th	R
6th	M
7th	C
8th	U
9th	L
10th	Q
11th	N
12th	I
13th	H
14th	B
15th	E
16th	S
17th	F
18th	G
19th	A
20th	J
21st	D

Figure 8-2. (continued)

There seem to be no formulae for determining the number of games in the tournament or the number of days required to play the tournament, given the number of entries. However, several listings up to sixteen entries have been calculated through counting, and they appear in Figure 8-3. D refers to the number of days required to play the tournament, and g/d indicates the number of games that can be played per day.

N	NUMBER OF GAMES	N	NUMBER OF GAMES
4	4	11	17
5	5	12	20
6	7	13	22
7	9	14	25
8	12	15	28
9	13	16	32
10	15		

2 g/d		3 g/d		4 g/d		5 g/d	
N	D	N	D	N	D	N	D
4	2	4	2	4	2	4	2
5	3	5	3	5	3	5	3
6	4	6	3	6	3	6	3
7	5	7	3	7	3	7	3
8	6	8	5	8	3	8	3
9	7	9	5	9	4	9	4
10	8	10	5	10	4	10	4
11	9	11	6	11	4	11	4
12	10	12	7	12	5	12	5
13	11	13	8	13	6	13	5
14	13	14	8	14	7	14	5
15	14	15	10	15	7	15	6
16	16	16	11	16	8	16	6

Figure 8-3.

REFERENCE

Mueller, Pat. *Intramurals: Programming and Administration,* fourth edition. New York: Ronald Press Company, 1971.

Chapter IX
ROUND ROBIN TOURNAMENT

THIS type of tournament involves the formation of leagues. Any number of entries above two can be in a league (although the usual range is from five to nine), and each entry plays every other entry in the league once.

A sample league of six entries appears below, and rounds of play refer to a circumstance where each entry is paired once with another entry. The first two rounds of play are illustrated. For this particular league, the number of rounds is five.

League A	Round 1	Round 2
1. Colts	Colts vs Steelers	Colts vs Rams
2. Bears	Bears vs Rams	Steelers vs Packers
3. Lions	Lions vs Packers	Bears vs Lions
4. Packers		
5. Rams		
6. Steelers		

ROTATION PATTERNS

To establish the full round robin schedule of games, a rotation pattern must be constructed. In the rotation pattern (Fig. 9-1) for the above-described league, each entry is represented by its corresponding number in the league lineup, i.e. Colts(1), Bears(2), Lions(3), and so forth. For the determination of all rounds beyond the first, one digit (top left corner) is held fixed as the other numbers are rotated one position counterclockwise. For an even number of entries, the number of rounds is always one less than the number of entries (N - 1 = 5). Each pairing of two numbers represents a game, and team names are substituted for the numbers in constructing the actual schedule.

Rd. 1	Rd. 2	Rd. 3	Rd. 4	Rd. 5
1 – 6	1 – 5	1 – 4	1 – 3	1 – 2
2 – 5	6 – 4	5 – 3	4 – 2	3 – 6
3 – 4	2 – 3	6 – 2	5 – 6	4 – 5

Figure 9-1.

The number of games in each round for an even-numbered league is found by dividing the number of entries by two ($N/2 = 3$). The number of games for each entry in the round robin schedule is one less than the number of entries ($N - 1 = 5$). When the top two seeds can be identified, they are placed in the numbers 1 and 2 positions in the league lineup because the (1 - 2) pairing allows them to play in the final round.

A rotation pattern for a league of seven entries is shown in Figure 9-2. For leagues with odd numbers of entries, the number of rounds equals the number of entries. Since one entry in each round cannot be paired with another entry, a bye (represented by the letter "B") must appear in each round. The B is placed in the top left corner of each round, and it is around the bye that each counter-clockwise rotation takes place. Only the pairings of two numbers represent games to be played. Those numbers paired with B's do not play in those specific rounds.

Rd. 1	Rd. 2	Rd. 3	Rd. 4	Rd. 5	Rd. 6	Rd. 7
B – 7	B – 6	B – 5	B – 4	B – 3	B – 2	B – 1
1 – 6	7 – 5	6 – 4	5 – 3	4 – 2	3 – 1	2 – 7
2 – 5	1 – 4	7 – 3	6 – 2	5 – 1	4 – 7	3 – 6
3 – 4	2 – 3	1 – 2	7 – 1	6 – 7	5 – 6	4 – 5

Figure 9-2.

The number of games in each round of an odd-numbered league is represented by the formula: $(N - 1)/2$, which results in three games for a league of seven. The number of games per entry in the round robin schedule is: $N - 1 = 6$.

For odd-numbered leagues, the top seed is placed in the second spot in the league lineup, and the second seed is placed in the last spot in the league lineup, because the pairing (2 - N) appears in the final round.

There may be occasion to establish round robin rotation patterns between two leagues, such that each entry in League A plays each entry in League B. An example, where League A has five entries and League B has four entries, is illustrated in Figure 9-3. League A is represented by Roman numerals, and League B is represented by Arabic numerals. When leagues are of unequal size, a bye is placed with those numerals representing the smaller league. Pairings in rounds beyond the first are determined by holding the numerals of one league constant, and rotating the numerals of the other league.

Rd. 1	Rd. 2	Rd. 3	Rd. 4	Rd. 5
B – I	B – II	B – III	B – IV	B – V
1 – II	1 – III	1 – IV	1 – V	1 – I
2 – III	2 – IV	2 – V	2 – I	2 – II
3 – IV	3 – V	3 – I	3 – II	3 – III
4 – V	4 – I	4 – II	4 – III	4 – IV

Figure 9-3.

TOURNAMENT PROBLEM-SOLVING

This section involves calculations one can make to determine, in advance of drawing a rotation pattern, the circumstances in which the tournament can be conducted. There are four factors that require consideration: (1) N, the number of entries, (2) the number of days needed to conduct the tournament, (3) the number of games available for play each day, and (4) the number of leagues and entries per league. By predetermining the first three listed factors, one can solve for the fourth.

All solutions to problems are based on the assumptions that no postponements are possible (or are replayed on weekends), and no entry plays more than once per day. That being the case, a day's schedule cannot exceed one round for each league.

The number of games required to complete a round robin league schedule, regardless of whether a league has an odd or even number of teams, is found by applying the formula:

$$\text{games} = \frac{N(N-1)}{2}$$

$$\text{if N} = 8, \text{then,}$$

$$\text{games} = \frac{8(8-1)}{2}$$

$$= 28$$

Note: Obviously, the higher the number of entries in a league, the greater the number of games required to complete a round robin schedule for that league. The total number of games can be reduced, however, by dividing the number of entries into more than one league. For instance, a round robin for a league of twenty-one entries requires the following number of games:

$$\text{games} = \frac{N(N-1)}{2}$$

$$= \frac{21(21-1)}{2}$$

$$= 210$$

That number can be substantially reduced by forming three leagues of five entries and one league of six entries. The total number of games now is:

league of six

$$\text{games} = \frac{6(6-1)}{2}$$

league of five

$$\text{games} = \frac{5(5-1)}{2}$$

$$= 15 \qquad\qquad = 10$$

$$\text{total games} = (3 \times 10) + 15$$

$$= 30 + 15$$

$$= 45$$

It is important to realize that, when more than one league is formed, such formation is done homogeneously; that is, the numbers of entries in the leagues cannot differ by more than one. For instance, it is undesirable to have two leagues of six and one league of eight. It is better to have two leagues of seven and one league of six.

Problem

Knowing the number of entries, the games available per day, and the number of days available to run the tournament, determine the minimum number of leagues that can be established and the number of entries in each league.

Example 1

Known: N = 23, 4 games/day, and 20 days available (regular season games only; no playoffs are considered).

Leagues are established in such a manner that the total number of games required for their round robin schedules comes close to, but does not exceed, the total number of games available for play. By establishing the fewest number of leagues possible, the number of available games that go unused can be kept to a minimum.

Step 1: Multiply the available days (20) times the games per day (4) to arrive at the total number of games available for regular season play.

$$\text{total games} = 20 \times 4$$

$$= 80$$

Step 2: Multiply the total number of games (80) by 2.

$$80 \times 2 = 160$$

Step 3: Divide the figure (160) found in Step (2) by N (23) to arrive at the number of games that can be offered each entry on an equal basis. Round off to the lower number.

$$160/23 = 6$$

Note: Although each entry is guaranteed six games, some entries may be able to play seven games (a circumstance that is determined by the calculations in the following steps).

Step 4: Subdivide N (23) until a row of figures appears, the numbers of which are less than or equal to the number of games that can be offered each entry plus one (7). The number (7) represents the number of entries in a league, which corresponds to six games per entry.

$$23$$
$$12 - 11$$
$$6 - 6 - 6 - 5$$

The number of figures in the final row (4) represents the maximum number of leagues with which a tournament may be formed, and which allows for the fewest number of wasted games. Since the minimum number of leagues is desired, it is necessary to determine if the formation of three leagues will result in a number of games that more closely approaches the total games available (80) but does not exceed them.

Step 5: Take the league with the smallest number of entries (5) and evenly (or nearly so) distribute the entries among the other three leagues. That process forms two leagues of eight and one league of seven. Determine the number of games required to complete round robin schedules for those leagues.

league of eight
$$games = \frac{8(8-1)}{2}$$
$$= 28$$

league of seven
$$games = \frac{7(7-1)}{2}$$
$$= 21$$

$$total\ games = (2 \times 28) + 21$$
$$= 56 + 21$$
$$= 77$$

Since seventy-seven games comes very close to, but does not exceed, the eighty games available, there is no need to proceed any further.

Answer: two leagues of 8 and one league of 7

Example 2

Known: N = 45, 6 games/day, and 22 days. In this case, a tournament champion will be determined by a single elimination playoff.

Step 1: Multiply the available days (22) times the games per day (6) to arrive at the total number of games available for play.

$$\text{total games} = 22 \times 6$$
$$= 132$$

Step 2: Multiply the total number of games (132) times two.

$$132 \times 2 = 264$$

Step 3: Divide that figure (264) by N (45) to arrive at the number of games per entry.

$$264/45 = 5$$

Step 4: Subdivide N (45) until a row of numbers appears, the numbers of which are less than or equal to the number of games per entry plus one (6).

$$45$$
$$23 - 22$$
$$12 - 11 - 11 - 11$$
$$6 - 6 - 6 - 5 - 6 - 5 - 6 - 5$$

Step 5: Take a league with the smallest number of entries (5), and form seven leagues (three leagues of 7 and four leagues of 6). Determine the number of games required to complete round robin schedules for those leagues.

league of six
$$\text{games} = \frac{6(6-1)}{2}$$
$$= 15$$

league of seven
$$\text{games} = \frac{7(7-1)}{2}$$
$$= 21$$

$$\text{total games} = (4 \times 15) + (3 \times 21)$$
$$= 60 + 63$$
$$= 123$$

The total games (123) comes close to but does not exceed the 132 games available.

Step 6: Two additional factors must now be considered — playoffs resulting from any league ties that might develop and the playoff between the league champions.

(a) For practical purposes, it is assumed that the maximum league tie that could develop would involve four entries. A single elimination playoff for four entries requires two rounds, or days, to play. It is further assumed that the maximum number of days that must be set aside to accommodate any combination of ties throughout all the leagues is two. Therefore, the number of games that must be added to the total games for league play (123) is a result of multiplying the number of days (2) times the games per day (6). None of these games may actually be played, but provision for their possible use must be made.

$$6 \times 2 = 12 \text{ games}$$

(b) A single elimination playoff for seven league champions is a three-round, three-day tournament. The number of games per day (6) is sufficient to cover each round in one day, because the number of games in the largest round is three. Therefore, the number of games that must be added to the total games for league play (123) is the result of multiplying the number of days (3) times the games per day (6).

$$3 \times 6 = 18 \text{ games}$$

Note: That figure includes the actual number of games played in the playoff (N - 1 = 6) and the number of games that could have been used but must go to waste (12).

The total number of games required to run the tournament is found by adding the numbers of regular season games (123), possible league-tie playoff games (12), and interleague playoff games plus those wasted (18).

$$\text{total games} = 123 + 12 + 18$$
$$= 153$$

That figure exceeds the number of games actually available for play (132), so the appropriate league structure temporarily reverts to that found in Step 4. However, five leagues of 6 and three leagues of 5 result in 105 games, plus the 30 games required for playoffs equals 135 total games, which is three too many. Thus, nine leagues of 5 must be formed by taking one entry from each of the five leagues of 6 (90 league games plus 36 playoff games equals 126 total games).

Answer: nine leagues of 5

Chapter X
LADDER TOURNAMENT

THIS tournament structure can be used for a ranking of the competitive abilities of players, as a means for pairing contestants of approximately equal ability in a perpetual system of play, and as a means of determining a champion.

Initially, it involves a listing of contestants, made at random or by a method of seeding. The listing temporarily ranks the contestants' abilities or performance relative to others on the ladder. Through the winning or losing of games played, the positions of contestants on the ladder are either raised or lowered. Winners move up, and losers move down.

The structure can be applied to formal and semiformal situations. The formal application is first described.

FORMAL STRUCTURE

Contestants are numerically listed by random draw or a combination of seeding and random draw. Figure 10-1 shows an example for seven entries. In the first round of play, the top-ranked contestant is given a bye, while the other entries are paired with each other, as illustrated by the dotted lines. The winners of contests played in round 1 are indicated to the right of each pairing, and the ranking of contestants in round 2 is the result of play in round 1.

Round 1	*Round 2*	*Round 3*

```
Round 1                  Round 2                    Round 3

1. Mason  --- bye         1. Mason -- ]              1. Mason  --- bye
2. Fife   -- ]            2. Bair  -- ] --- Mason    2. Bair   -- ]
3. Bair   -- ] --- Bair   3. Fife  -- ]              3. Hansan -- ] ---
4. Hansan -- ]            4. Hansan -- ] --- Hansan  4. Fife   -- ]
5. Mack   -- ] --- Hansan 5. Mack  -- ]              5. Thye   -- ] ---
6. Thye   -- ]            6. Thye  -- ] --- Thye     6. Mack   -- ]
7. Adrian -- ] --- Thye   7. Adrian --- bye          7. Adrian -- ] ---
```

Figure 10-1.

When two entries play, and the entry with the higher ranking looses, those two entries switch positions for the following round. When the contestant with the higher ranking wins, the two contestants maintain their relative positions. For example, Fife lost to Bair in round 1, so they switch positions for round 2. Hansan defeated Mack in round 1, so their positions are maintained. Therefore, one can move up the ladder only by defeating a higher ranked opponent.

Since the top entry received a bye in the first round, play is structured in the second round so the bottom entry receives a bye. Therefore, the top and bottom contestants alternate byes round by round. That procedure is employed so the same two contestants never play each other twice in a row. The final ranking of contestants is established after completion of a predetermined number of rounds of play.

In Figure 10-2, the flow of play for an even number of entries is demonstrated. Note, again, the alternating fashion in which contestants are paired round by round. That prevents the meeting of two contestants in consecutive rounds, and it allows contestants the consistent opportunity to play higher or lower ranked entries. For example, if round 2 positional pairings were made in the same manner as in round 1 (1 vs 2, 3 vs 4, 5 vs 6, 7 vs 8), the same contestants would play each other again. Further, if such a procedure were maintained throughout the rounds of play, contestants would never move more than one place ranking, up or down. However, an obvious problem with this procedure is that, in every other round, two contestants do not play. An alternate method for an even number of entries is described below and illustrated in Figure 10-3.

Round 1

1. Mason ---]--- Mason
2. Fife ---
3. Bair ---]--- Hansan
4. Hansan ---
5. Mack ---]--- Mack
6. Thye ---
7. Adrian ---]--- Stubbs
8. Stubbs ---

Round 2

1. Mason --- bye
2. Fife ---]--- Fife
3. Hansan ---
4. Bair ---]--- Mack
5. Mack ---
6. Thye ---]--- Thye
7. Stubbs ---
8. Adrian --- bye

Round 3

1. Mason ---]---
2. Fife ---
3. Hansan ---]---
4. Mack ---
5. Bair ---]---
6. Thye ---
7. Stubbs ---]---
8. Adrian ---

Figure 10-2.

Round 1

1. Mason ---]--- Mason
2. Fife ---
3. Bair ---]--- Hansan
4. Hansan ---
5. Mack ---]--- Mack
6. Thye ---
7. Adrian ---]--- Stubbs
8. Stubbs ---

Round 2

1. Mason ---]--- Hansan
2. Hansan ---
3. Mack ---]--- Fife
4. Fife ---
5. Bair ---]--- Bair
6. Stubbs ---
7. Thye ---]--- Adrian
8. Adrian ---

Round 3

1. Hansan ---]---
2. Mason ---
3. Fife ---]---
4. Bair ---
5. Mack ---]---
6. Adrian ---
7. Stubbs ---]---
8. Thye ---

Figure 10-3.

In each round of play, the pairings will always be the same (1 vs 2, 3 vs 4, 5 vs 6, 7 vs 8). The winners of contests in a particular round of play must always move to a higher ranking for the following round of play; conversely, losers must always drop in ranking.

Although this method eliminates the prospects for byes, there are two distinct disadvantages, as compared to the previously described procedure. First, in each round of play, the possibility exists that contestants will move up or down two place rankings instead of just one. For example, as a result of the first round of play (Fig. 10-3), Hansan and Stubbs advance two place rankings for round 2. As a result of play in round 2, Mack drops two places, and Adrian advances two places. Second, one contestant can jump ahead of another contestant without having to play that contestant. For instance, the playing of round 2 (Fig. 10-3) finds Mack and Bair changing positions on the ladder without their having played each other. In the procedure described in Figure 10-2, there is a more orderly exchange of positions on the ladder, because positional changes are the result of direct competition between the contestants involved.

SEMIFORMAL STRUCTURE

Participants listed on the ladder are responsible for arranging their own matches and repositioning their names on the ladder board. The ladder board might consist of a series of slots, into which name plates can be placed, removed, and replaced. The method (random, seeding) by which players are initially positioned on the board is of no particular consequence.

Matches are formed through a challenge system. Except for the player at the top, any player may challenge another player to a match, such that the player being challenged is no more than two positions above the challenger. If the challenger wins the match, the two players switch positions on the board. If the challenger loses the match, positions remain as they were. Sample matches are illustrated in Figure 10-4. The positional changes shown in Figure 10-5 reflect the fact that Jones defeated Smith, Barnes defeated Haynes, and Andrus defeated Garner.

1. Jones	1. Jones	1. Harvey
2. Harvey	2. Harvey	2. Jones
3. Smith	3. Smith	3. Smith
4. Haynes	4. Barnes	4. Barnes
5. Barnes	5. Haynes	5. Andrus
6. Garner	6. Andrus	6. Haynes
7. Andrus	7. Garner	7. Garner
Figure 10-4.	Figure 10-5.	Figure 10-6.

After losing, a player must accept a challenge from a person in a lower position (last player excepted). Winners may challenge players in higher positions. Within those guidelines, matches may be arranged as shown in Figure 10-5. The results of play are illustrated in Figure 10-6 (Harvey defeated Jones, Smith defeated Barnes, and Andrus defeated Haynes). Figure 10-6 also reveals possible match-ups for the next round of play.

Under this structure, play may continue until general interest is lost. Players may be dropped from, or added to, the ladder as circumstances dictate. Added players are placed at the bottom of the ladder.

Section II

TOURNAMENT SCHEDULING

Chapter XI
THE ENTRY PROCESS

ENTRY DEADLINES

ENTRY deadlines must be established for those sports that require schedules to be formed. The deadlines must be coordinated with the sports' proposed first days of play, such that sufficient time exists to form the schedules and communicate them to participants. Typically, the entry period begins one week before the deadline.

To avoid possible confusion and misplacement of entries, no entries should be accepted before the entry period begins. During the entry period, the office and staff should be prepared and mobilized to efficiently accept entries. That efficiency cannot be expected at times far in advance of the deadline.

It is important to adhere to entry deadlines rather strictly. Inevitably, late entries are submitted or requested, but it is necessary to establish a certain discipline in the operation of the program. Otherwise, deadlines, rules, and regulations become clouded, and they lose meaning when not enforced consistently. Furthermore, it is impractical to expect the staff to begin its scheduling process over to accommodate late entries. There has to be a cut-off, so the staff can get on with its work. Perhaps, a good rule is this:

> Late entries are accepted up to the point that the staff begins the scheduling process. If the entry is accepted, a late entry fee is imposed. A person submitting a late entry has no rights. Whether or not a late entry is accepted is left completely to the discretion of the staff. It is the responsibility of participants to meet entry deadlines, so no complaints are justifiable if a late entry is not accepted.

For activities that do not require schedules and are conducted on a meet basis, such as track, swimming, special events, etc., entry deadlines are probably not needed. Entries can be taken on the day of the event, just before it begins. There is at least one type of scheduling process for team sports that does not require deadlines but employs lifelines instead (Match-Up Scheduling, see Chapter 15). The scheduling process begins as soon as enough teams are entered, and subsequent entries, regardless of when made, are incorporated into the schedule as soon as possible. Obviously, such a system is not usable for programs that have leagues and championships. It is designed to match up teams on the basis of competitive parity and is simply a means for providing play for teams that are not overly concerned about winning or losing.

ENTRY FORMS

It is common policy to have all participants or team captains submit an entry form as the official request for scheduling consideration. Separate mimeographed forms can be prepared for team sports and individual/dual sports; or, one form could be designed for both.

The type of information requested on the forms might vary from sport to sport and program to program. All forms should solicit the following information from participants: Name of Sport Entered, Name of the Team or Organization Represented, Name of Participant(s) or Team Captain, Address and Phone Number of Person Entering. As a refinement, it may also be valuable to request listings of all team members (social security numbers might be included), the days of the week and times of the day on which the entry absolutely cannot play, and the other teams (coed, for instance) of the same sport, or other sports that are concurrently scheduled, on which a significant number of people play.

A team sport entry form is illustrated in Figure 11-1. A combination team and individual/dual sport entry form is shown in Figure 11-2. It should be indicated in clear terms that the information is to be printed or typed. Perhaps, a regulation would be in order with regards to the circumstances in which an entry is refused due to illegibility.

MANFRED HIGH SCHOOL
INTRAMURAL SPORTS

TEAM ENTRY FORM

PRINT OR TYPE ALL INFORMATION

NAME _____   TEAM NAME _____

DIVISION: GIRLS ___   BOYS ___   CO-ED ___   SKILL LEVEL: A ___ B ___ C ___

TEAM CAPTAIN

NAME _____

ADDRESS _____

ZIP CODE _____   PHONE _____

INDICATE BELOW ANY OTHER TEAMS (IN SAME
SPORT OR OTHER CONCURRENTLY SCHEDULED
SPORT) ON WHICH A SUBSTANTIAL NUMBER OF
YOUR PEOPLE PLAY. AN EFFORT WILL BE MADE
TO AVOID SCHEDULING CONFLICTS.

SPORT   DIVISION   TEAM NAME

ROSTER

BY CHECKING THE APPROPRIATE BOXES BELOW, INDICATE WHEN YOUR TEAM CANNOT PLAY					
TIME	MON	TUES	WED	THUR	FRI	SUN
4:00						
5:00						
6:00						
7:00						
8:00						
9:00						

Figure 11-1.

```
                    BROOKLYN COLLEGE
                    INTRAMURAL SPORTS

                       ENTRY FORM


TOP HALF FOR TEAM SPORTS ONLY
──────────────────────────


SPORT _____  TEAM NAME _____


DIVISION:  MEN ___  WOMEN ___  CO—ED ___       SKILL LEVEL:  A ___   B ___


                    CAPTAIN                         ENTRY FEE STATUS
                    ───────                         ────────────────

NAME _____              PAID _____

ADDRESS _____          NOT PAID _____

ZIP CODE _____  PHONE _____      WITHDRAW FROM
                                                    ACCOUNT _____
```

If there are days and times of day that you <u>ABSOLUTELY</u> cannot play, make
mention of them here. The director will do his best to accommodate you,
but no promises.

```
────────────────────────────────────────────────────────────────────


BOTTOM HALF FOR INDIVIDUAL AND DUAL SPORTS
──────────────────────────────────────────


SPORT _____  DIVISION:  MEN ___  WOMEN ___  CO—ED ___


NAME _____       ENTRY FEE STATUS
                                                   ────────────────
ADDRESS _____             PAID _____

ZIP CODE _____  PHONE _____           NOT PAID _____

                                                   WITHDRAW FROM
                                                       ACCOUNT _____
TEAMMATE'S NAME _____
(for dual sport)
```

Figure 11-2.

ENTRY PROCEDURE

There are two basic ways to take entries. Participants can deposit entry forms in a specific area of the office; or, participants must submit entries directly to a staff member. The latter method is the better of the two, but it involves one distinct problem — someone must be constantly in the office to take entries. If that is not feasible, certain hours per day may be scheduled as an entry period.

What needs to be avoided is a nonstructured system, whereby participants might think it all right to slip entries under doors, lay them on desks, or otherwise put them in places where they might get lost. It is a touchy situation when a person who had submitted an entry that had subsequently been misplaced, comes into the office after a schedule has been drawn up; that person will be upset because he/she or the team entered is not on the schedule. If entries are permitted to be submitted without a staff person present, there must be a clearly identifiable place in which to deposit them — such as a container with a slot. Even then, a certain degree of entry mishandling is likely, and the matter of collecting entry fees is difficult to standardize with that process.

Very few mistakes and misunderstandings should occur when the staff takes entries. Participant questions can be answered; entry forms can be checked for illegible printing, failure to fill in all necessary information, unacceptable team names; and entry fee submission can be verified before final acceptance. Immediately upon acceptance of an entry, certain minimal information should be transferred to a master entry list — Team Name or Organization, Division of Play, Team Captain or Name of Individual Entry, Address, and Phone Number. The master list can be considered as the official record of entries. If an entry form gets misplaced, at least the existence of the entry is recorded on the master list. If, after the entry deadline, someone claims to have submitted an entry that cannot be found, it can be assumed with reasonable assurance that the entry was never properly submitted, if no record of it appears on the master list.

For those schools or communities that have a significant number of organizations, entries are best recorded in a card-filing system. Figure 11-3 shows an organization entry card. It lists all the sports, and provides space for the names and phone numbers of those individuals entered or responsible for those sports. It is particularly valuable to have collected on one card all of an organization's entries for an individual or dual sport. As will be demonstrated in Chapter 12 (Scheduling Single Elimination Tournaments), those entries must be appropriately separated in the tournament bracket, so entries from the same organization do not meet each other prematurely in the tournament. Possible errors and much sorting time are saved by having organizational entries already listed together.

ORGANIZATION:		ADDRESS:		PHONE:
SPORT	PARTICIPANTS' NAMES	SPORT	TEAM CAPTAIN	
TENNIS SINGLES	1. _____ 2. _____ 3. _____	FOOTBALL		
BADMIN SINGLES	1. _____ 2. _____ 3. _____	BASKETBALL		
		VOLLEYBALL		
GOLF SINGLES	1. _____ 2. _____ 3. _____	SOFTBALL		

Figure 11-3.

As master lists are devised, and entry forms accepted, it is wise to provide immediately for any categorizing of entries that must be done before the scheduling process can begin. For instance, separate master lists are drawn for divisions of men, women, and coed, and entry forms for those divisions are deposited in separate places. The entry forms for such categories could also be color coded. If schedules are to be mailed to participants, an envelope could be attached to the entry forms, and a request made that they be addressed by entrants.

As a source of program funds, entry fees can be established for some or all activities. The amount of the fee might depend on whether the competition is individual/dual or team, and the number of contests that can be guaranteed per entry. A team sport on a round robin schedule can elicit a higher entry fee than an individual sport conducted on a single elimination basis.

Even if funds are not required for the program, entry fees could be established for the purpose of "weeding out" those people who might make frivolous entries and, subsequently, forfeit scheduled contests. The payment of an entry fee guarantees, to some extent, that an entry is really interested in the program and will likely meet schedule commitments. Those sports that do not require the printing of a schedule need not have an entry fee. Submitted entry fees could be considered as forfeit fees and returned to participants upon completion of their schedules without forfeits.

Entry fee collection for organizations, or any group that intends to enter sports consistently under the same name, can be handled in two ways. Instead of having groups pay fees every time they enter, they could pay a flat fee that covers entry in all activities for the year, or they could deposit a substantial sum of money into an account with the intramural office, from which fees are withdrawn as the need arises.

At the conclusion of the entry period, a final check of the entry forms against the master list should be made.

Chapter XII
SCHEDULING SINGLE ELIMINATION TOURNAMENTS

THREE methods are described. The first is usable for indoor sports, which have little chance of having contests postponed due to unforeseen circumstances. Thus, the full tournament schedule can be established and printed with specific dates, times, and playing areas indicated. The other two methods are more flexible; therefore, they may be used for outdoor, as well as indoor sports.

PROCEDURES FOR ESTABLISHING A PRINTED SCHEDULE

Step 1: Establish the starting date of the tournament, the times of the day on which it will be conducted, and the number of playing areas available. For purposes of illustration, the following is assumed:

$$N = 39, \qquad 3 \text{ playing areas,} \qquad 3 \text{ times per day}$$

Thus, 9 contests may be played per day.

Step 2: Calculate the number of days required to complete the tournament under the assumed circumstances.

$$
\begin{array}{cccccc}
1 & 2 & 3 & 4 & 5 & 6 \\
\hline
7 & 16 & 8 & 4 & 2 & 1 \\
 & -2 & & & & \\
\cline{2-2}
 & 14 & & & & \\
\hline
1 & 2 & 1 & 1 & 1 & 1 \\
\end{array}
$$

(7 DAYS)

Structure 7

105

Step 3: Establish the days on which the tournament will be run, and list them, along with available times and play areas, in chronological order for future reference.

Note: It is assumed that seven days are available for play. If not, Step (2) would involve the determination of the number of contests that must be played per day in order to complete the tournament in, for example, six days.

Structure 8

Step 4: Determine the breakdown of N for a seeded bracket. Arrange numbers to accommodate eight seeds.

Structure 9

Note: If the schedule is to be mimeographed, or otherwise placed on 8½ x 11 inch pieces of paper, a modified procedure is required for any number of entries that exceeds thirty-two. Such a number of entries requires more than one piece of paper, so the bracket must be divided into "flights." A flight consists of a number of entries between 7 and 17. It is a separate single elimination bracket, and the winners of all flights are placed in another single elimination bracket to complete the tournament. The modified procedure (Step 4b) does not alter the single elimination context of the total tournament. It is simply a means for dividing the bracket into workable sections.

Step 4b: Look at the breakdown of N, and identify the row of numbers that contains numbers between 7 and 17.

10 - 10 - 10 - 9

That means four flights will be drawn — two on the first page and two on the second. Also, a championship flight for the four flight champions will be drawn at the bottom of page two.

  Now, look at the bottom line of the breakdown in Step (4). It must be divided into four sections, with each section containing four numbers. Taking them in the order presented, the flight set-up for the tournament is shown below.

Flight 1 : 3 - 2 - 2 - 3
Flight 2 : 3 - 2 - 2 - 3   first page

Flight 3 : 3 - 2 - 2 - 2
Flight 4 : 3 - 2 - 2 - 3   second page

Step 5: Sketch worksheet brackets, with two flights per page. The final bracket of flight winners is placed at the bottom of the second page. Figure 12-1 illustrates the worksheet. Number, from 1 to N, each line of each flight bracket. N, in this case, refers to the number of entries in each flight, so N cannot exceed 16. Also, number, from 1 to N, the final bracket of flight winners. The numbers, there, refer to flight numbers; so, the winner of flight 3 is placed on the third line of the final bracket.

Step 6: Between the lines of each pairing, identify the day, date, time and court or field number, as shown in Figure 12-1. If insufficient space is available for all that, the day and court or field number may be eliminated. The date and time are the bare essentials, along with the location, which can be identified at the top of the schedule.

FLIGHT 1

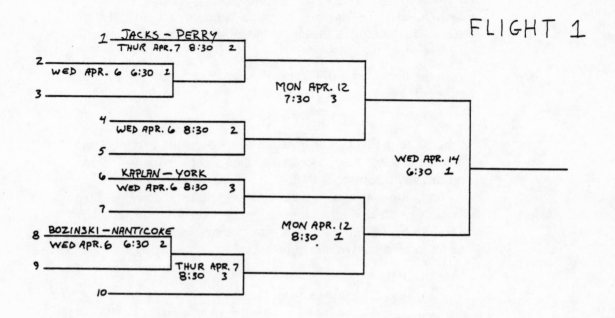

FLIGHT 2

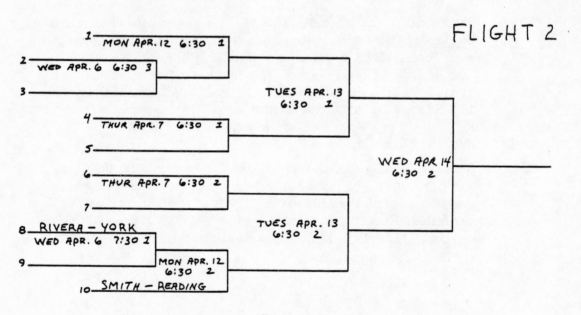

Figure 12- 1.

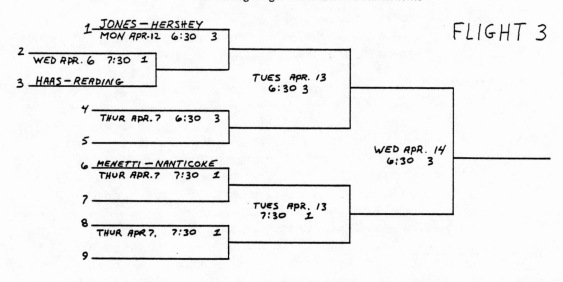

FLIGHT 3

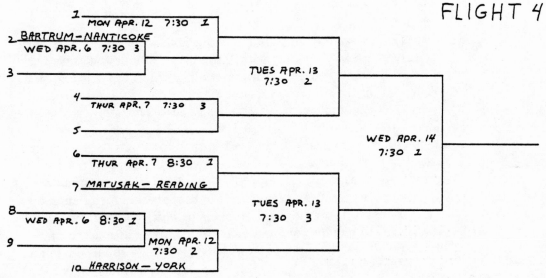

FLIGHT 4

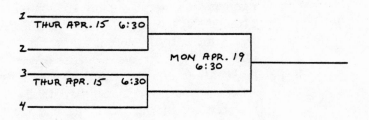

CHAMPIONSHIP FLIGHT

Figure 12-1. (continued)

Step 7: The names of entries are placed on lines of the brackets.

Note: Since single elimination tournaments are employed most often for individual or dual sports, such as badminton, entries refer to names of people rather than names of teams. Further, two situations require attention. A tournament may or may not involve people who are affiliated with organizations. If the tournament is "open," the placement of entries in the bracket may be done by random draw (after the seeds are placed). If organizations are involved, and there are more than one entry per organization, the procedure is a little more complex. Therefore, the organizational situation will be described.

A. Based upon past performances or other criteria, entries are ranked in seeded order, and their names and organizations are placed on the appropriate lines of the bracket. Last names may be all that are necessary. A dash separates the entry's name from the organization's name. See Figure 12-1. The first four seeds are placed on Line 1 of Flight 1, Line 10 of Flight 4, Line 10 of Flight 2, and Line 1 of Flight 3.

B. Entries of the same organization must be listed or gathered together for easy reference. Starting with those organizations that have the most entries, and proceeding in descending order, unseeded entries are placed on the bracket in semirandom order. Random placement is used, except that entries from the same organization are separated so their meeting is delayed for as long as possible. For instance, if an organization has four entries, one entry is randomly placed in each quarter of the bracket. No two of the entries could possibly play each other before the semifinals of the tournament. As entries are placed on the bracket, indicate beside their names on the entry list or form the flight numbers in which they appear.

C. Several sets of numbers are needed for the purpose of random draw. The "flight" set has numbers from 1 to N, where N equals the number of flights. The "line" sets run from 1 to N, where N equals the number of lines in the largest flight. The number of line sets equals the number of flights, and each set corresponds to a specific flight number. For the placement of each entry, two numbers are drawn. From the flight set, a number is drawn to determine the flight in which the entry is placed. If the flight number drawn is incompatible with those for other entries of the same organization, numbers are continually drawn until a usable flight has been determined. After each entry has been placed, all numbers in the flight set are replaced for the next drawing. Then, a number is drawn from the line set of the appropriate flight to determine the exact line of the flight on which the entry is placed. Again, numbers are drawn until a usable number appears. After the drawing for each entry, numbers are not replaced in the sets, since their usability is terminated.

D. Below are examples of some entry placements, as they appear in Figure 12-1.

NAME	ORGANIZATION	FLIGHT SET	LINE SET
Menetti	Nanticoke	3	6
Bartrum	Nanticoke	4	2
Bozinski	Nanticoke	1	8
Kaplan	York	1	6
Rivera	York	2	8
Haas	Reading	3	3
Matusak	Reading	4	7

Step 8: With all entries placed on the worksheets, a check is made to be sure each entry has been properly designated in the tournament. One by one, each entry on the list is checked off, as his/her name is found on the bracket. The flight numbers, which were written beside the entries' names upon original placement, are referred to for quick location on the bracket.

Step 9: The bracket is ready for transfer to the final product, whether that be a single copy (on paper or large cardboard) or many mimeographed copies. For mimeographing, the bracket must be drawn on stencils. Each worksheet page translates to one stencil. Bracket lines are drawn first, using the matching numbers on the sides of the stencils as horizontal guides. Then, the entries and schedule information are typed on and between the lines. Equipment required: ruler, stencil pen, correction fluid, a sheet with four vertical lines (placed under the stencil, and used to guide the length of the horizontal lines for each round), typewriter, and a mimeograph machine.

An example of a finished product appears in Figure 12-2. A standard rule is employed for this type of schedule to accommodate those players that cannot make a scheduled time. Contests may be played at a mutually agreed upon time and place, such that the contest is completed before the winner would next play in the succeeding round. Therefore, the flow of the tournament is not delayed. The tournament director must approve such arrangements in advance. Also, regardless of the type of scheduling method employed, a procedural regulation must be established with regards to allowing or not allowing another player to substitute for a player already on the schedule. When organizations are involved, a member of the same organization usually may substitute, provided he/she is not otherwise listed on the bracket. No outright switches of players can be made. For an "open" tournament, a substitution must be approved by the player who would receive the forfeit.

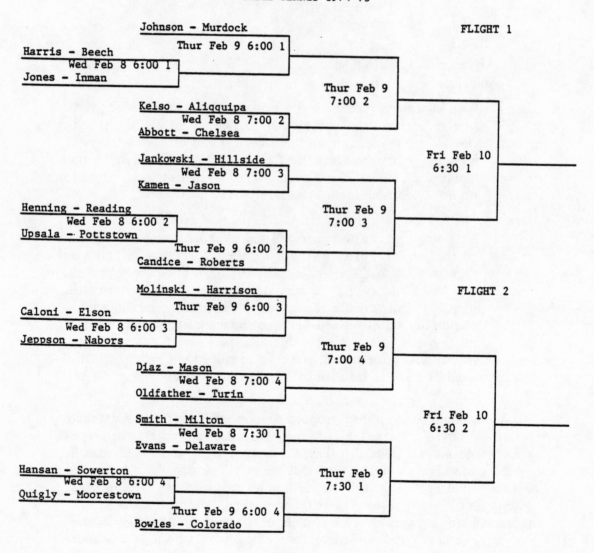

BANCROFT HIGH SCHOOL
INTRAMURAL ATHLETICS

TABLE TENNIS 1974-75

Figure 12-2.

FLIGHT 3

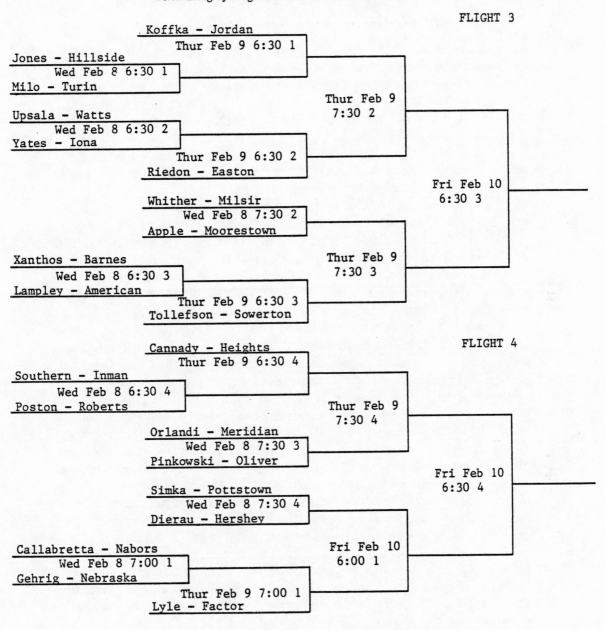

FLIGHT 4

CHAMPIONSHIP FLIGHT

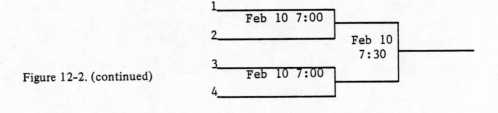

Figure 12-2. (continued)

PRINTED SCHEDULE FOR FLEXIBLE PLAY

A tournament bracket can be constructed without designating specific dates and times for play. Instead, a deadline date is established, and a contest is to be played by that date. Opponents are responsible for contacting each other; arranging the day, time, and place of the contest; and reporting the results to the tournament director. Winners then identify their next opponents, and proceed as before.

A small bracket is illustrated in Figure 12-3. Note that full names and telephone numbers are made evident for ease of contact. The bracket, itself, is constructed as described in the previous section.

This scheduling method is particularly useful for situations in which the varied academic and work schedules of participants do not conveniently allow for their being available for play during restricted days and times of the day. Contests are played at the convenience of the participants, rather than to a set schedule. Also, the need for reserving the playing areas for a specific amount of time each tournament day is eliminated; supervision of the tournament is unnecessary. Theoretically, the tournament runs itself.

However, that is not the usual case. Usually, at least one contest every round is unplayed by the deadline date. That puts a burden on the tournament director to contact participants and find out why the contest was not played. That often turns into a hassle, as players blame each other for not getting together, or inclement weather had consistently made postponement of intended play necessary. All sorts of rules can be devised in an attempt to avoid such a situation, but they do not work consistently because there are all sorts of legitimate exceptions to the rules. A typical rule would have both players meet at the intramural office at a specific time on the deadline date so, in the presence of the tournament director, the contest may be scheduled. Thus, if the contest still goes unplayed, the tournament director can more confidently arrive at a judgment as to who violated the agreement, because he was there when the agreement was made.

That system still is not fullproof, and one or both participants might not be able to comply with the meeting rule because of some other commitment. So, a decision must be made to: (1) declare a winner based on the information available, (2) declare a double forfeit, or (3) extend the deadline and somehow get the contest played. The first two alternatives are bound to make people unhappy, and it flies in the face of the supposed participatory aims of sport, but they do keep things on schedule. The third avenue probably allows the contest to be played, but the tournament is held up, and the deadline dates and any rules for meeting them become mushy, if not meaningless.

Another disadvantage of this scheduling arrangement is that players lose the "sense" of being in a tournament, since the playing of contests is isolated from the others. It is probably more fun and interesting to play in the same area where other contests are taking place. Other players can be watched, and the prospects of socialization are enhanced.

MONTROSE JUNIOR HIGH SCHOOL
INTRAMURAL ATHLETICS

GIRL'S TENNIS-SINGLES
1975-76

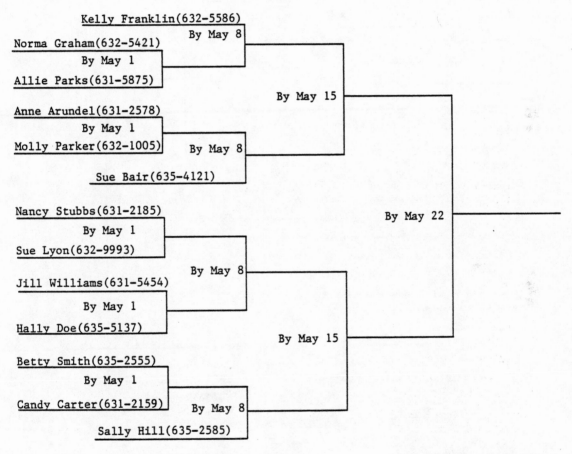

Contact your opponent immediately, and arrange to play by the deadline date shown.

Winners report scores to the tournament office.

689-3340

Matches may be played on any regulation tennis court. A match consists of the best of three sets.

Figure 12-3.

SCHEDULE WITH PRINTING OR NONPRINTING OPTIONS

A tournament bracket is structured as shown in Figure 12-4. Each contest is designated by a parenthesized number. It is that number which is referred to in the scheduling process.

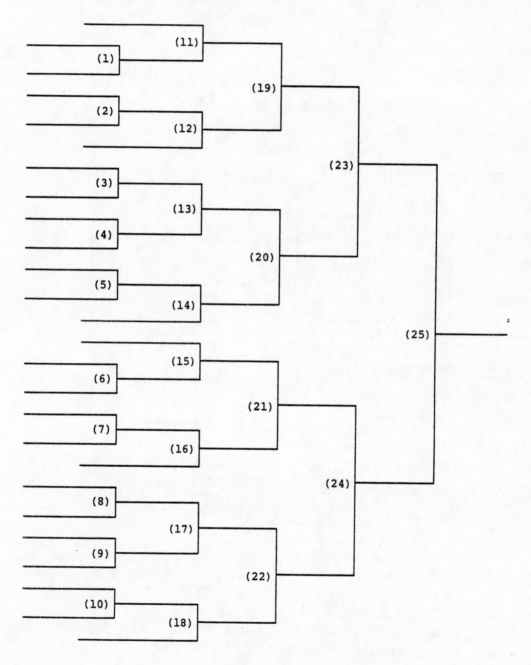

Figure 12-4.

There are two methods of handling the scheduling. Figure 12-5 illustrates a set schedule that is rather easily revised in the event postponement is necessary. The schedule refers to the tournament bracket shown in Figure 12-4. This, as well as the previously described scheduling methods, allows all participants to determine, well in advance of the tournament's first contest, their individual playing times. That, in turn, permits people the opportunity to plan other activities around their schedules. This method also establishes a contingency schedule that automatically takes effect, without the need for contacting players, in the event a whole day's play is postponed. If further scheduling is required, the match numbering system simplifies communication of the revised schedule.

All matches have been numbered in parentheses. To determine playing times, check the match numbers with the schedule below.

Saturday	*Sept . 11*	*Sunday*	*Sept. 12*	*INCLEMENT WEATHER CONTINGENCIES*
10:00 am	1,2,3	12:30 pm	19,20	Should Saturday matches be rained out, play
11:15 am	4,5,6	1:45 pm	21,22	will begin at 12:30 pm on Sunday, and play
12:30 pm	7,8,9	5:00 pm	23,24	will follow the schedule below. Revised
1:45 pm	10,11,12	arranged	25	schedules for the next weekend will be
3:00 pm	13,14,15			printed and mailed.
4:15 pm	16,17,18			

Should Sunday matches		12:30 pm	1,2,3
be rained out, revised		1:45 pm	4,5,6
schedules for the next		3:00 pm	7,8,9
weekend will be printed		4:15 pm	10,11,12
and mailed.		5:30 pm	13,14,15
		6:45 pm	16,17,18

Figure 12-5.

The second scheduling method, using the same tournament bracket (Fig. 12-4), is shown in Figure 12-6. No more than three days of play are scheduled at a time, and they are posted with the bracket in one or more locations on school grounds. When one day of play is completed, another day of the schedule is added. This method allows for the postponement of contests, without having to reestablish the schedule for all the remaining contests. Only three days of play need be rescheduled. Although considerable flexibility is offered by this scheduling method, it has two distinct disadvantages. Players cannot forsee their playing times any farther in advance of three days, and they must continually call the tournament office or go to the schedule-posting location to determine their next playing times. Also, confusion may result from postponements, since the postponed games must be played on the next available scheduling day (usually the next day of the week). People who were involved with the established games for the next three days suddenly have to readjust to playing on the following days. The people scheduled for the second and third days must always be alert for postponements on days that precede them, because their schedules are, in turn, altered.

All matches have been numbered in parentheses. To determine playing times, check the match numbers with the schedule below. In the event matches are rained out, they will be played on the next available day for scheduling.

MONDAY, APRIL 15		*TUESDAY, APRIL 16*	
3:30 pm	1,2,3	3:30 pm	10,11,12
5:00 pm	4,5,6	5:00 pm	13,14,15
6:30 pm	7,8,9	6:30 pm	16,17,18

WEDNESDAY, APRIL 17	
3:30 pm	19,20
5:00 pm	21,22

Figure 12-6.

Chapter XIII
SCHEDULING DOUBLE ELIMINATION TOURNAMENTS

THE upper, or championship, brackets of all double and triple elimination and consolation tournaments are single elimination tournaments of their own. Therefore, the brackets are structured as previously described, but they are not scheduled in the same way, because the lower-bracket contests must be considered. Even though their structures differ somewhat, all consolation and multiple elimination tournaments are scheduled in a similar manner. Double elimination is described.

Double elimination tournaments that have a number of entries approaching or exceeding sixteen usually require two or more pieces of 8½ by 11 inch paper. The first sheet (Fig. 13-1) contains the upper bracket, and the second sheet (Fig. 13-2) contains the lower bracket and final two games between the survivors of the two brackets. The number of entries is twenty-one, and four contests may be scheduled per day.

Take note that the first two rounds of the upper bracket are completely scheduled before the first round of the lower bracket receives attention. That is the procedure because the losers of the first two rounds in the upper bracket play each other in the lower bracket's first round. Also note that care must be taken not to schedule an entry for play more than once per day. There are places in the tournament that do not allow for sequential scheduling. For instance, in the first round of the lower bracket, the contest between losers 12-13 was circumvented to schedule the losers 4-6. Since lower 13 already played a game in the upper bracket on October 6, it could not again be scheduled for October 6. To the extent possible, the first two rounds of the lower bracket are completed before the third round of the upper bracket is scheduled.

There comes a point in every tournament when the number of contests that can be played per day exceeds those that can (or should) actually be

UPPER BRACKET

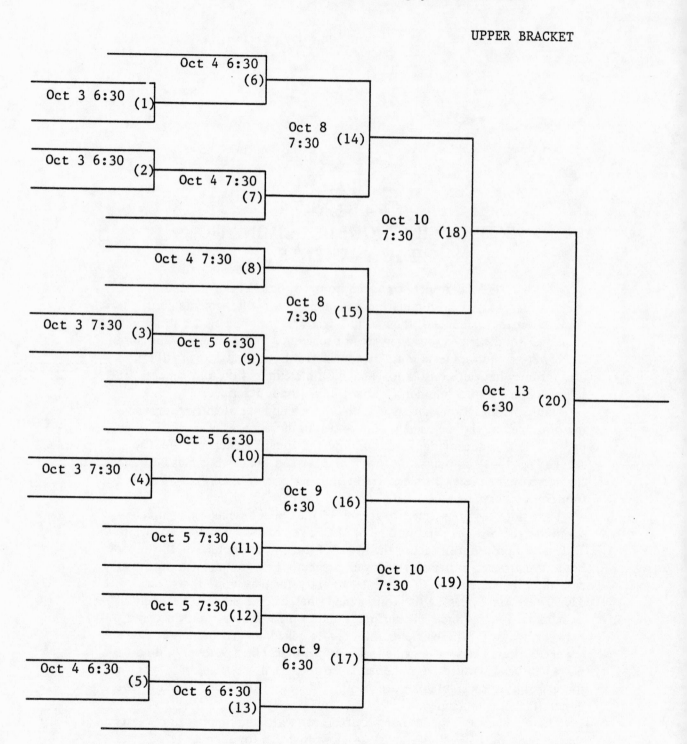

Figure 13-1.

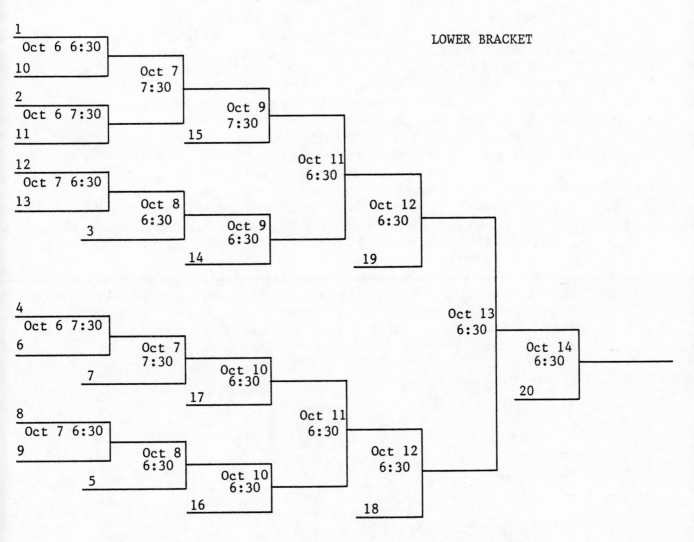

LOWER BRACKET

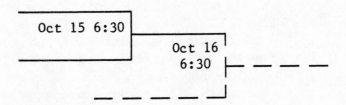

Figure 13-2.

scheduled. Such a situation occurs for the first time in the fourth round of the loser's bracket (Fig. 13-2). Two contests are scheduled for October 11. Two more are available for play, but there are only three contests that could conceivably be scheduled. Two of them (fifth round of lower bracket, involving upper-bracket losers 18 and 19) cannot be scheduled, because it would involve entries playing more than once per day. The last contest of the upper bracket (20) could be scheduled, but the winner (and loser, for that matter) would have to wait a long time before playing again. It is better to space things out as equitably as possible, so certain entries do not get stale due to a long lay-off. So, the prudent course of action is to not schedule a third contest on October 11, even though it is available. That will not in any way delay the flow of the tournament or require more days to complete it. The typical procedure is to schedule the final contest of the upper bracket with the second-to-last contest of the lower bracket (October 13).

The tournament runs from October 3 to October 16 (14 days). That corresponds to the calculation that could have been made prior to scheduling the tournament. With N = 21 and 4 games/day, the number of games in the tournament equals 41, and the appropriate ratio is 7 - 15. Twenty-six games remain, and they can be played in seven days. Seven plus seven equals 14 total days. The figures below show the calculation in practical form.

$$
\begin{array}{r}
41 \\
7-15 \\
+7 \quad \overline{4\,|\,26} \\
\underline{} \\
\boxed{14} \quad 7
\end{array}
$$

Structure 10

There are occasions when double elimination tournaments are conducted on a short-term basis (a weekend, for example) for special events. Such a tournament appears in Figure 13-3. It is a two-day basketball tournament, so the rule that no entry plays more than once per day must become that no entry plays more than once per hour. Further, no two entries ever have to play games in successive hours. That rule presents yet another scheduling consideration.

For the tournament in Figure 13-3, two games can be scheduled per hour. Note that the lower bracket game between the losers of upper bracket games 2 and 9 cannot be scheduled at 2:00 PM, as the normal scheduling sequence would have it. Since game 9 of the upper bracket was played at 1:00 PM, at least one hour must be left open for either of those two teams to rest before having to play again. Thus, the lower-bracket game is scheduled for 3:00 PM. For the same reason, the third round of the upper bracket is played (4:00 PM) before the third round of the lower bracket (5:00 PM).

There is only one place in the tournament where two teams must play games in consecutive hours. It occurs between the fourth and fifth rounds of the lower bracket (10:00 AM and 11:00 AM). That is done to speed up the flow of the tournament. Also, note that the rest period before the final two games is only one-half hour. Again, that is done for expediency.

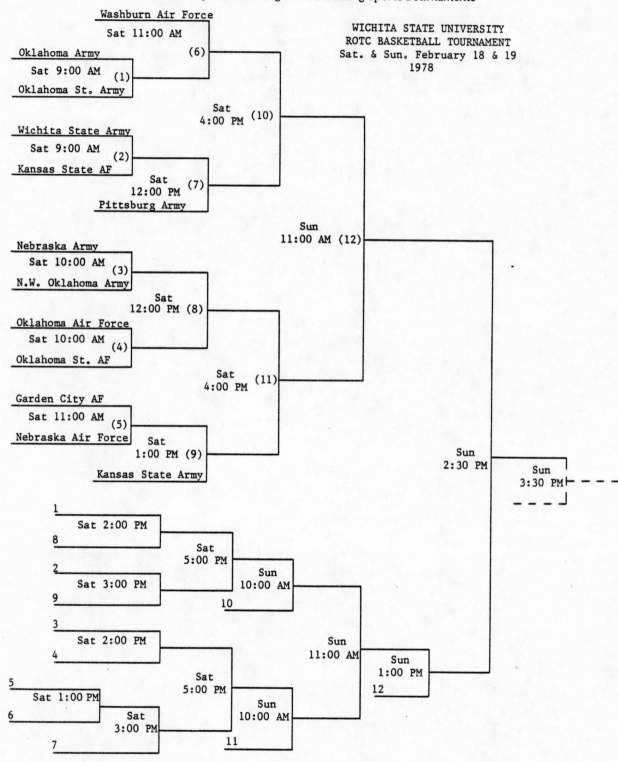

Figure 13-3.

Chapter XIV
SCHEDULING ROUND ROBIN
TOURNAMENTS

THIS type tournament is mostly utilized for team sports. The objective is to determine the number of leagues and teams per league that fit the available circumstances. Then, teams are assigned to leagues, and the schedule is formed. Three pieces of information are necessary: the number of entries (N = 62), the number of games that can be played per day (6), and the number of days on which games can be played (57).

Step 1: Keeping in mind that provisions must be made for league ties and playoffs, and employing the method for determining the number of leagues and teams per league described in the section on tournament problem-solving, it is determined that four leagues of ten and two leagues of eleven can be formed. In certain circumstances maximum league sizes may be undesirable. As the number of teams in a league becomes larger, more teams will quickly get the idea, after a few games, that they have no chance at winning the championship or making the playoffs. Therefore, the possibility exists that a larger number of forfeits would occur, toward the end of the season, in a large league than in a smaller league. A choice must be made between the possibilities of more participation or more forfeits.

Step 2: League rotation patterns are drawn up for ten and eleven entries. Actually, mimeographed worksheets of rotation patterns for all league possibilities should already be prepared and on file for immediate use. Figure 14–1 illustrates a worksheet for a league of six entries. The double horizontal lines separate rounds of play. For the situation at hand, four worksheets for ten entries and two for eleven entries are procured for use.

LEAGUE

1.
2.
3.
4.
5.
6.

TEAMS	DATE	TIME	PLAY AREA
1-6			
2-5			
3-4			
1-5			
6-4			
2-3			
1-4			
5-3			
6-2			
1-3			
4-2			
5-6			
1-2			
3-6			
4-5			

Figure 14-1.

Step 3: Based upon previous performances or other factors, teams are identified for seeding purposes. The league winners of the previous year should be placed in separate leagues. For even-numbered leagues, the top two seeds are placed in the top two positions on the worksheet; and, for odd-numbered leagues, the top seed is placed in the second spot and the second seed is placed in the last spot. Those two procedures guarantee the meeting of the top two seeds for their last game of the regular season. Other teams are assigned to leagues by a random draw from a pool of six numbers (one for each league), and they are written on the worksheet.

Step 4: Dates, times, and play areas are assigned to games on the six league worksheets. As they are assigned, they are checked off, as being used, on a chronological master list of available days, times, and play areas. Usually, a full round of one league is scheduled before another league's games are scheduled. For instance, all five games in Round One of League A (Fig. 14-2) are scheduled before any games in League B are scheduled. First-round games for all the leagues are scheduled before returning to League A to schedule second-round games. The orderly process of scheduling each league round by round may be altered somewhat if there are definite advantages and disadvantages to playing on certain days, times of day, and play areas. A rotation system may have to be devised to equalize those scheduling factors among all the teams. As such, rounds of play and games within rounds may not appear on the schedule in chronological order. That does not change the nature of the schedule, it just makes the scheduling process more complicated. Scheduling proceeds on that basis until all games are scheduled. The full schedule for League A is shown in Figure 14-2.

Step 5: The final product – the schedules that are either posted on bulletin boards or delivered to team captains – can take two forms: each league's schedule can stand by itself, as formed on the worksheet, or a master schedule can be formed that incorporates games from all leagues in the chronological sequence of daily play. In the first instance, teams are given only their own league schedules, which saves paper and is most appropriate when very large numbers of teams must be scheduled. However, a master schedule must be drawn up for the tournament director's use, so the total flow of the tournament can be viewed. However, and as will be illustrated later, such a master schedule need not be as involved as the master schedule that would be printed for general use. Even though more paper is required for a master schedule, the convenience of its use usually dictates its preference over the other method, as long as the number of entries is within reason. It makes little sense to send every team a ten-page schedule when their own league's schedule can be available on one sheet of paper.

LEAGUE A

1. Donora	6. Allentown
2. Beaver Falls	7. Farrell
3. Lycoming	8. Charleroi
4. Palmyra	9. Springfield
5. Red Lion	10. Somerset

TEAMS	DATE	TIME	PLAY AREA
1-10	Mon. 2/8	6:30	1
2-9	" "	"	2
3-8	" "	"	3
4-7	" "	"	4
5-6	" "	7:30	1
1-9	Wed. 2/10	7:30	3
10-8	" "	"	4
2-7	" "	8:30	1
3-6	" "	"	2
4-5	" "	"	3
1-8	Tue. 2/16	6:30	1
9-7	" "	"	2
10-6	" "	"	3
2-5	" "	"	4
3-4	" "	7:30	1
1-7	Thur. 2/18	6:30	4
8-6	" "	7:30	1
9-5	" "	"	2
10-4	" "	"	3
2-3	" "	"	4
1-6	Mon. 2/22	7:30	2
7-5	" "	"	3
8-4	" "	"	4
9-3	" "	8:30	1
10-2	" "	"	2

TEAMS	DATE	TIME	PLAY AREA
1-5	Thur. 2/25	6:30	2
6-4	" "	"	3
7-3	" "	"	4
8-2	" "	7:30	1
9-10	" "	"	2
1-4	Tue. 3/2	6:30	4
5-3	" "	7:30	1
6-2	" "	"	2
7-10	" "	"	3
8-9	" "	"	4
1-3	Thur. 3/4	7:30	1
4-2	" "	"	2
5-10	" "	"	3
6-9	" "	"	4
7-8	" "	8:30	1
1-2	Wed. 3/10	6:30	3
3-10	" "	"	4
4-9	" "	7:30	1
5-8	" "	"	2
6-7	" "	"	3

ALL GAMES PLAYED IN THE SOUTH GYM OF THE FIELD HOUSE.

Figure 14-2.

Individual league schedules can be written or typed on a mimeographed worksheet (Fig. 14-2), and delivered or picked up by team captains. A notation must be made on the schedule as to the location of the play fields or courts. The tournament director must then compile a master schedule, part of which appears in Figure 14-3. Four play areas are scheduled in each of three time slots. Games are consistently assigned to play areas in numerical sequence. Each game is indicated by a league letter and a numbered rotation pairing. The first game of the schedule (Monday, Feb. 8) involves teams 1 and 10 of League A. To quickly determine which teams those numbers represent, one refers to a master list of leagues (Fig. 14-4). The first game is between Donora and Somerset.

DATE	6:30	7:30	8:30	6:30	7:30	8:30	DATE
MON 2/8	A 1-10	A 5-6	B 4-7	B 10-8	C 1-9	C 4-5	THUR 2/11
	A 2-9	B 1-10	B 5-6	B 2-7	C 10-8	D 1-9	
	A 3-8	B 2-9	C 1-10	B 3-6	C 2-7	D 10-8	
	A 4-7	B 3-8	C 2-9	B 4-5	C 3-6	D 2-7	
TUES 2/9	C 3-8	D 2-9	E 1-10	D 3-6	E 2-7	F 1-8	MON 2/15
	C 4-7	D 3-8	E 2-9	D 4-5	E 3-6	F 2-7	
	C 5-6	D 4-7	E 3-8	E 11-9	E 4-5	F 3-6	
	D 1-10	D 5-6	E 4-7	E 1-8	F 11-9	F 4-5	
WED 2/10	E 5-6	F 4-7	A 2-7	A 1-8	A 3-4	B 2-5	TUES 2/16
	F 1-10	F 5-6	A 3-6	A 9-7	B 1-8	B 3-4	
	F 2-9	A 1-9	A 4-5	A 10-6	B 9-7	C 1-8	
	F 3-8	A 10-8	B 1-9	A 2-5	B 10-6	C 9-7	

Figure 14-3.

LEAGUE A	LEAGUE B	LEAGUE C	LEAGUE D
1. Donora	1. Radnor	1. Johnstown	1. Shamokin
2. Beaver Falls	2. Nanticoke	2. Erie	2. Hazelton
3. Lycoming	3. York	3. Hoban	3. Hershey
4. Palmyra	4. Bellefonte	4. Meyers	4. Lebanon
5. Red Lion	5. Tioga	5. Coughlin	5. Lancaster
6. Allentown	6. Penncrest	6. Catasaqua	6. Sharon
7. Farrell	7. Hickory	7. Norristown	7. Perkiomen
8. Charleroi	8. Schenley	8. Tamaqua	8. Uniontown
9. Springfield	9. Bradford	9. Haverford	9. Montrose
10. Somerset	10. Altoona	10. Harrisburg	10. Berwick

Figure 14-4.

A master schedule suitable for general distribution is depicted in Figure 14-5. Only the first and last pages are shown. Note three features of the schedule: (1) For identification purposes, the appropriate league letter appears to the left of all games. (2) For ease of reading, horizontal lines separate days of play. (3) The single elimination playoff between league winners appears at the bottom of the last page. The lines on which league winners will be placed are indicated, and they were determined by random draw.

Note: Large university programs often contain several divisions of play (dormitory, fraternity, sorority, independent, and so forth). Since teams do not play across divisions, each division has its own master schedule. The tournament director may want to establish a super master schedule that identifies, for quick reference, the divisions and leagues that are playing on particular days. The actual typing of the schedule on a mimeograph stencil is done from the league worksheets. Starting with League A (Fig. 14-2), and proceeding through the other leagues one round at a time, scheduling information from the worksheets is transferred to the stencil. Team names are substituted for the numbered rotation pairings. As each game is typed on the stencil, it is checked off on the worksheet, to prevent accidental duplication.

Step 6: When the master schedules have been mimeographed and collated and are ready for distribution, two things should be done on each team's schedule. One, the team name is underlined, as it appears in the league listing. That identifies whose schedule it is, for the joint benefit of the sports staff and any team captain who forgot the name of the team under which he/she entered. Two, in the left margin, all the team's games are identified by a check mark. That allows team captains to readily determine their schedules of games. Also, in the course of checking off games, the staff can note any scheduling mistakes.

MANOOSA STATE UNIVERSITY
IM-REC SPORTS

BASKETBALL 1978-79

LEAGUE A	LEAGUE B	LEAGUE C
1. Newman Center	1. SAE III	1. SPT's
2. Physician's Asst.	2. Beta Donuts	2. Buddy's Boys
3. Fairmount Towers	3. Kappa Sig IV	3. Kwanza Harambee I
4. Beta III	4. Beta IV	4. Horatio's
5. Beta V	5. Phi Delt IV	5. Eagles
6. Phi Delt III	6. Kappa Sig III	6. Stagetrotters

LEAGUE D	LEAGUE E	LEAGUE F
1. Unknowns	1. College Inn	1. Kwanza Harambee II
2. B-2 Bouncers	2. Linebackers	2. Rockets
3. Brennan Celtics	3. Piatt Street Five	3. Marauders
4. Trippers	4. F Troop	4. Salt & Pepper
5. Bachelors	5. Tri-F's	5. AA
6. Ballcrushers	6. Die Wunderkinder	6. Bombers
	7. Panthers	7. A.F. ROTC

ALL GAMES ARE PLAYED IN MITTLE GYM.

LG.		DATE	TIME
D	Unknowns vs Ballcrushers	Wed. Feb. 4	6:30 PM
D	B-2 Bouncers vs Bachelors	" " "	7:30
D	Brennan Celtics vs Trippers	" " "	8:30
C	SPT's vs Stagetrotters	Mon. Feb. 9	6:30
C	Buddy's Boys vs Eagles	" " "	7:30
C	Kwanza Harambee I vs Horatio's	" " "	8:30
F	Kwanza Harambee II vs A.F. ROTC	Tue. Feb. 10	6:30
F	Rockets vs AA	" " "	7:30
F	Marauders vs Salt & Pepper	" " "	8:30

CONTINUED ON NEXT PAGE

Figure 14-5.

LG.		DATE	TIME
E	Linebackers vs Panthers	Mon. Mar. 29	6:30 PM
E	Piatt Street vs Wunderkinder	" " "	7:30
E	F Troop vs Tri-F's	" " "	8:30
F	Rockets vs A.F. ROTC	Tue. Mar. 30	6:30
F	Marauders vs Bombers	" " "	7:30
F	Salt & Pepper vs AA	" " "	8:30
B	SAE III vs Beta Donuts	Wed. Mar. 31	6:30
B	Kappa Sig IV vs Kappa Sig III	" " "	7:30
B	Beta IV vs Phi Delt IV	" " "	8:30

CHAMPIONSHIP PLAYOFF

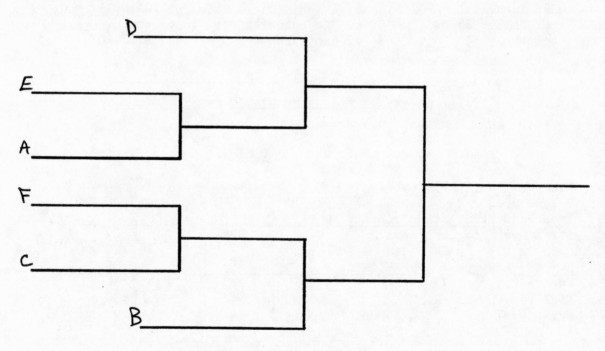

Figure 14-5. (continued)

VARIATIONS

Thus far, the scheduling methods described do not take into account some circumstances that might better be addressed by making certain alterations in standard scheduling procedures. What if a sport is typically entered by more teams than can be handled by existing facilities? That is particularly applicable to bowling, where only a set number of alleys and time periods are available. What if many teams would like to play all their games at a specific time(s) on a specific day(s)? What if the delay between the entry deadline and the start of play is too long because schedules must be formed and distributed?

Various scheduling systems can be devised to solve one or all of those problems. The scheduling method featured here takes all those considerations into account.

Step 1: Evaluate the situation with regards to the maximum number of play areas available, on what days they are maximally available, and for how many time periods per day they are maximally available. As those are considered, also consider the availability of participants to play at those times, and consider the availability of officials and supervisory personnel to staff the games comfortably. Make sure that days are set aside for playoffs and postponements. From those deliberations, arrive at a master schedule of games that could be played during the regular season.

Step 2: Form leagues that have predetermined schedules on the basis of playing on a certain day(s) at a specific time(s). The objective might be to have all League A games played at 6:30 PM on Mondays. League formation is dependent on two factors: the number of play areas available per time period and the number of anticipated entries (or the number of entries that can be reasonably handled on a first-come, first-served basis).

All sorts of variations are possible. If, for instance, four play areas are usable, all leagues could have eight or nine entries, and any particular league could be designated to play at a specific time on one or more days per week. With four play areas, two leagues of four or five each could also be accommodated. The number of entries per league and the number of days each league plays per week is influenced by the total number of anticipated entries, but the basic concept — each team playing all its games on a specific day(s) of the week and at a specific time of the day — is unaffected. Figure 14-6 illustrates two league schedules, as they would be distributed to team captains. Each of the two leagues plays in a circumstance involving three play areas, but one league has six entries and the other league has seven entries. Note that an odd-numbered league requires two more weeks to play than its corresponding even-numbered league.

LEAGUE A   MONDAYS   6:30 PM

1. BOMBERS	DATE	COURT 1	COURT 2	COURT 3
2. LIONS	10/4	1-6	2-5	3-4
3. TIGERS	10/11	6-4	2-3	1-5
4. JAYS	10/18	5-3	1-4	6-2
5. BEARS	10/25	4-2	5-6	1-3
6. EAGLES	11/1	1-2	3-6	4-5

LEAGUE A   MONDAYS   6:30 PM

1. BOMBERS	DATE	COURT 1	COURT 2	COURT 3
2. LIONS	10/4	1-6	2-5	3-4
3. TIGERS	10/11	7-5	1-4	2-3
4. JAYS	10/18	6-4	7-3	1-2
5. BEARS	10/25	5-3	6-2	7-1
6. EAGLES	11/1	4-2	5-1	6-7
7. TWISTERS	11/8	3-1	4-7	5-6
	11/15	2-7	3-6	4-5

Figure 14-6.

Step 3: Assuming that the first day of play is Monday, October 4, as indicated by the schedules in Figure 14-6, the entry deadline could be established as being Friday, October 1. On a first-come, first-served basis, team captains submit an entry form to the intramural office, and select the league in which they would like to play. The selection is based, of course, on the day of the week and time of day that the league plays. The team name is written in two places: once on a master set of league schedules to be kept in the intramural office, and once on the prepared mimeographed schedule sheet (which includes all dates and pairings of play) that is immediately given to the team captain. If the team is the fourth to be entered in a league, its name is placed in the fourth position, and the other three team names are filled in on the schedule. If the team captain wishes to know which other teams are in the league, he/she must return to the intramural office at a later time to find out. A team can immediately procure its schedule upon entry, but it will not know all the other teams it plays until all league positions have been filled.

The predetermined set of leagues is formed on the assumption that the eventual number of entries will always be larger than can be accommodated by the league structures. Therefore, the master schedule of games, determined in Step 1, can be completely used up for the initial set of leagues only if one is sure that the number of entries will be large enough to fill the leagues, and some entries will have to be turned away or put on a waiting list. If sufficient entries are not assured, the initial set of leagues should not encompass all scheduling possibilities. For instance, Fridays are not made available for entry until all other leagues are filled or 9:30 PM games on any day are held back until other leagues are filled.

Step 4: Post one or more master lists of league schedules in appropriate places in the sports office or elsewhere on school grounds.

PLAYOFF SYSTEMS

The simplist and most often used playoff method is to have league winners engage in a single elimination tournament to determine the divisional or overall champion. League ties may be broken through playoffs or by a system of priorities, such as (1) which team won in head-to-head competition and (2) total points scored in all games minus points scored against.

Any of the elimination, consolation, and playback tournaments, previously described, can be employed for playoffs. There are several variations as to who gets into the playoffs. It need not be just the league winners. More teams can be guaranteed entry into the playoffs in an effort to sustain the playing interest of those teams that might forfeit their last few scheduled contests because they no longer have a chance at the league championship.

Any number of playoff systems could be devised, and several are cited here.

(1) For any given number of entries, league sizes can be reduced, which would increase the number of leagues and the number of league winners. Further, double round robins could be played within the small-sized leagues, and the winner of each round of play (if different) can be advanced to the playoffs.

(2) Place any number of league entries (from 2 to N) into the playoffs, and seed them on the basis of their league records. For instance, winners of Leagues A, B, C, and D receive byes or play first-round games against any combination of last-place finishers in the same leagues, such that teams of the same league do not meet each other in the first round. Second-place league finishers are matched against second-to-last-place finishers, and so forth.

(3) Have classification playoffs, placing league finishers of like standing in separate brackets, with their own championships. That is, all league winners compete for the "A" championship, all second-place finishers compete for the "B" championship, and so forth.

(4) At the end of the regular season, all teams with a .500 or better record play off for the right to meet the first-place team for the league championship. The winner of the playoff between the .500 or better teams must beat the first-place team twice in succession to win the league championship. The first-place team need win only once to win the championship. A playoff between league champions is then held.

REFERENCE

Fabian, Lou. "Scheduling Intramural Programs for Commuter Colleges," *Journal of the National Intramural-Recreational Sports Association*, 2:49-52, May, 1978.

Chapter XV
RANDOM AND MATCH-UP SCHEDULING PROCEDURES

THERE are some intramural programs, or parts of programs, that have developed in such a way that championships in team sports no longer exist. The idea is to concentrate on participation rather than winning. As such, league structures must be avoided, and teams are paired so no two of them play the exact same schedule of other teams. That prevents any sort of meaningful comparison of team records. Two systems have been devised, and they are detailed in subsequent pages.

RANDOM SCHEDULING

The first consideration is to determine the number of total possible games that can be scheduled.

Step 1: Determine the number of days (27, for example) on which games can be played.

Step 2: Determine the number of playable games per day by multiplying the number of available courts or fields (3) times the number of playing times per day (2).

$$3 \times 2 = 6 \text{ games/day}$$

Step 3: Multiply the number of days available (27) times the number of games playable per day (6).

$$27 \times 6 = 162 \text{ total games}$$

The second consideration is to determine the number of games that can be scheduled for each team.

Step 1: Establish the number of teams entered (22, for example).

Step 2: Multiply the number of total games (162) by two.

$$162 \times 2 = 324$$

Step 3: Divide that number (324) by the number of teams (22) to find the number of games allowed each team. Round off to the lower number.

$$324/22 = 14 \text{ games/team}$$

The third consideration involves the establishment of the rotation pattern from which team pairings can be selected. Since the number of teams (22) is even, all rounds of play find each team paired with another (such is not the case for an odd number of teams). Since each team is to be scheduled for fourteen games, only fourteen of the total twenty-one rounds (columns) of the rotation pattern need be structured for team pairings. The first three rounds are depicted in Figure 15-1.

1	2	3
1-22	1-21	1-20
2-21	22-20	21-19
3-20	2-19	22-18
4-19	3-18	2-17
5-18	4-17	3-16
6-17	5-16	4-15
7-16	6-15	5-14
8-15	7-14	6-13
9-14	8-13	7-12
10-13	9-12	8-11
11-12	10-11	9-10

Figure 15-1.

By random draw, each team is assigned to a number in the pattern. To form the printed schedule, numbered pairings (using team names) are placed into the predetermined schedule of available days and times of day, exactly as they were for round robin scheduling. The final random schedule looks just like a round robin schedule, except that, on the first page, teams are listed without league affiliation and, on the last page, there is no provision for a playoff.

When the number of teams is odd (25, for example), each team *is not* paired with another team in each of the rounds. In each round, one team must always receive a bye. So, for any number of rounds that is less than the total number in the rotation pattern, some teams play more games than other teams.

After the number of games per team (4, in this case) has been determined, the full rotation pattern for the odd number of teams must be established. When the number of teams is rather large, as it is here, a short-cut can be employed. The number of teams (25) must be split into two sections (7 and 18, for example). Because of the necessity to avoid the formation of a round robin schedule, so league champions cannot be determined, the split must be made such that a full rotation pattern for each section result° in a number cf games per team that is greater than the actual number of games (4) to be scheduled for each team. Consistent with the purpose of the split, the odd-numbered section is smaller than the even-numbered section, so the full rotation pattern is structured with a relatively small number. The sections of seven and eighteen teams both result in a number of games per team greater than four (6 and 17, respectively).

For the section of eighteen teams, four columns of the rotation pattern are established in a fashion similar to that already illustrated for the twenty-two team example. For the section of seven teams, the rotation pattern is shown in Figure 15-2. The letter "B" indicates a bye. Notice that the numbers start with 19, because the first 18 numbers formed the other section of teams.

1	2	3	4	5	6	7
B—25	B—24	B—23	B—22	B—21	B—20	B—19
19—24	25—23	24—22	23—21	22—20	21—19	20—25
20—23	19—22	25—21	24—20	23—19	22—25	21—24
21—22	20—21	19—20	25—19	24—25	23—24	22—23

Figure 15-2.

As indicated by the parallel lines, team pairings are determined by reading horizontally across the columns. In each horizontal round, every team is paired with two other teams. Therefore, in order to form a schedule of four games per team, the team pairings of any two horizontal rounds must be selected. The printed schedule is established in the manner previously described.

MATCH-UP SCHEDULING

There are at least four problems that evolve with the printing of a full season's schedule, particularly when no championships are at stake. First, when teams drop from sight and have no intention of playing their remaining games, undesirable "holes" in the schedule occur. Consequently, those teams that show up to play, and have no one to play, may in turn forfeit future games. In that way, forfeits lead to other forfeits, and the possible "snowball" effect ruins a program. Second, a major goal of a program that has no championships is to provide teams with equalized competition, so play can be interesting and enjoyable, relative to the negative aspects of lopsided scores. With a printed schedule, there is no opportunity to adjust team pairings during the course of the season, when future mismatches become apparent.

Third, when inclement weather forces the postponement of a day's schedule, those games must be rescheduled at times that are usually undesirable — weekends or days beyond the season's last scheduled day. Fourth, any teams that miss the entry deadline cannot be placed on the schedule, except in unusual circumstances.

The solution to those problems rests with the design of a flexible, match-up scheduling procedure. Such a procedure involves day-to-day scheduling, with communication of the schedule to players by means of a recorded telephone message and/or typed schedules that are posted on school grounds. Specifically, here's how it works.

As before, the days of play, the playing times per day, and the courts or fields available are predetermined. A block record form (see Fig. 15-3), including all teams, is constructed. If the number of teams is too large, more than one form, including appropriate sections of teams, can be constructed. An example for seven teams is illustrated.

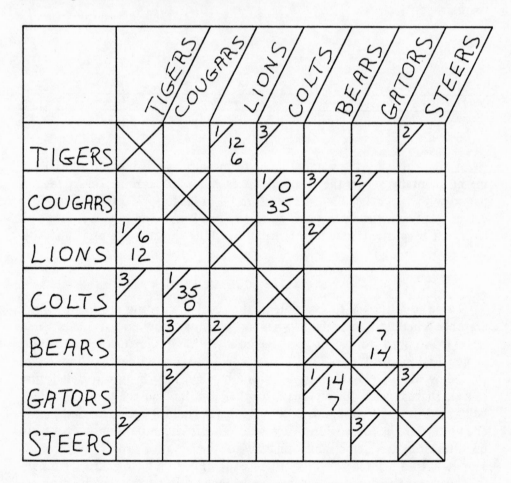

Figure 15-3.

Since teams are listed twice, each team pairing (Tigers vs Lions, for instance) is connected by two blocks on the form. Each time two teams are paired, the number (1, 2, 3, 4, etc.) of the day in the schedule, not the date, is recorded in the upper left corner of the two appropriate blocks. The notations serve as references that aid the scheduling process. Initially, the first three days of the schedule are formed, and they are verbally recorded on a tape that is hooked to a special telephone line and/or are typed and posted. Each team captain is responsible for determining his/her own schedule by dialing the telephone number that connects to the recording or by looking at the posted schedule.

After each day of play, scores are recorded in the two blocks that correspond to each game. The form is read horizontally; so, in the above example, the Lions lost to the Tigers (6-12). Also, another day's schedule of games is determined, indicated as such on the block form, and recorded on the tape and/or posted. The tape must be wiped clean every day, so the previous day's schedule can be eliminated, and the current schedule of the next three days is recorded in chronological order. Beyond the first few days of play, teams are paired to achieve competitive parity, which is based on previous scores and personal observation and evaluation, by the sports staff, of relative team strengths.

When a team forfeits a game, it is not again scheduled for another game until the captain informs the sports office of the team's desire and intention to play future games. Should a team forfeit a second time, it will no longer be scheduled.

Entry deadlines are not established; instead, an entry lifeline exists. Entries are accepted at any point beyond the entry lifeline, and the first three days' schedule is formed as soon as enough teams enter. Subsequent entries are incorporated into the scheduling process at the earliest opportunity. Those teams that enter soon after the lifeline date can expect to be scheduled for more games than those teams that enter substantially later.

When it is necessary to postpone a day's schedule, a new tape is recorded, with the postponed games being listed on the third day of the three listed on the tape.

The whole scheduling process for a particular sport obviously ceases when the predetermined final day of the sport season is reached.

Progressive Scheduling[1] is a variation of the Match-Up Scheduling method, and is utilized by Washington State University. It is employed as a system that leads to championships.

After entries are taken, each team's name is placed on an index card. Cards are placed in a container, and they are drawn two at a time to form games. Schedules are formed and communicated to participants. The result

---

[1] Epperson, Steve and Steve Schmitz, "Progressive Scheduling Method," *Proceedings of the National Intramural-Recreational Sports Association Conference.* 28:64-66, 1977.

of each team's game is recorded on its index card, and the team's progressive record is kept on the card. After each round of play, cards with like records are placed in separate containers (all teams with 1-0 records in one container, and teams with 0·1 records in another container). The next round of play is drawn from the separate containers. Should odd numbers of cards be in the containers, games can be scheduled between teams of similar records, thus avoiding byes. As play proceeds, round by round, teams are continually paired on the basis of their records.

At the end of the regular season schedule, teams with like or similar records engage in single or double elimination championship playoffs. Even teams with poor records are given the opportunity to play in the post-season tournament.

Chapter XVI
MISCELLANEOUS SCHEDULING CONSIDERATIONS

THE TYPE OF TOURNAMENT TO USE

THERE are five potential objectives in conducting a tournament. A champion is to be determined by the most valid means possible, the place rankings of other entries are to be established, each team or individual is to be afforded maximum playing opportunities, games are to be scheduled on the basis of competitive parity, and teams or individuals are to be scheduled for a nearly equal number of contests. Some tournament structures provide for the satisfaction of several objectives, while others can meet only one or two of them. Choice of a tournament depends not only on the achievement of desired objectives, but, most influentially, on the number, age, sex, and skill of the people playing, the type of sport, whether it is of an individual or team nature, the number of contests that can be played per day, and the number of days available for play. The calculations described in the section on tournament problem-solving are preparation for determining which tournament is most suitable for use when the number of entries, available games per day, and number of days available are considered. The usefulness of the different tournaments is subsequently discussed.

Single elimination requires the fewest number of contests to reach an acceptable champion. Participation is severely limited, however, because one loss eliminates an entry from the competition. A premium is placed on winning to continue participation, which is to the advantage of the better players. The sudden-death nature of the tournament might induce entries (especially teams) to play desperately, roughly, and unfairly.

Since single elimination requires a minimum number of contests, it is most useful in situations where a large number of entries must play in limited circumstances. That situation usually presents itself more for individual/dual sports than for team sports. The nature of the facilities often influences the play of individual/dual sports in the single elimination structure. If, for example, the badminton courts overlap the basketball courts (rendering them useless during a badminton tournament), the number of people actually participating in an activity is probably less during badminton play than basketball play, since team sports involve more people than do individual or dual sports. Also, the number of courts available for sports such as tennis, handball, and badminton are almost always too few to meet the demand for their general use. To "tie up" the courts with any kind of lengthy tournament (beyond single elimination), thus reducing opportunities for unstructured play, might be unjustifiable.

Theoretically, single elimination play offers fewer chances of forfeit occurrence. Since one loss eliminates an entry from play, each entry only has one opportunity to forfeit; in other tournaments (especially round robin), each entry can accumulate forfeits. It is interesting to observe that individuals tend to forfeit more often than do teams. That would be a good reason to conduct individual sports in single elimination tournaments, regardless of the availability of time and facilities.

When elimination tournaments are used for outdoor sports, weather delays often cause inconvenient scheduling problems. It is risky to print a complete schedule, with all the dates and times, because postponed contests, with few exceptions, must be played the next available day if the tournament is to continue in orderly fashion. In that event, the remaining dates printed on the schedule, and possibly the times of day, become inoperative. The type of single elimination tournament that might work rather efficiently for outdoor sports is the one in which deadline dates are set for the playing of each round, and contestants arrange their own matches.

In double elimination structures, each entry is assured of playing at least two contests, thus the degree of total participation is increased over that which would result from single elimination play. A more acceptable champion than in single elimination is determined, because one loss does not eliminate an entry from the tournament. An entry can play that one bad game, and still have a chance at the championship.

Double elimination requires about twice as many games and time periods to play as does single elimination, with the last three contests requiring three separate time periods to play. An annoying circumstance with this and other types of multiple elimination and consolation tournaments arises when a forfeit occurs in the upper or championship bracket. If the forfeiting individual or team does not appear for scheduled play in the lower or consolation bracket, the same entry is responsible for a second forfeit. Furthermore, if a double forfeit should occur in the upper bracket, byes must be written in the two spots that those two entries were to have been placed — in the following round of the upper bracket and the appropriate round in the lower bracket.

Thus, that one double forfeit is responsible for three scheduled contests not being played.

Other advantages, disadvantages, and uses for double elimination are simiłar to those expressed for single elimination.

Triple elimination tournaments guarantee entries the playing of three contests. The number of contests required to complete a triple elimination tournament is comparable to that for round robin play. For instance, if N = 12, triple elimination requires thirty-five contests, while round robin, when the entries are split into two leagues of six, requires thirty-one games (including a playoff between league winners). Since round robin play, in that situation, guarantees each entry five contests, instead of just three, it would seem that round robin is the more advantageous tournament. Further, because round robin play provides for the meeting of every other entry in the league, a more valid champion would seem to be determined.

Neither proposition is necessarily true. Particularly in the individual/dual sports, round robin play is more subject to forfeits than is triple elimination. In the example cited, an entry can be responsible for three and five forfeits in triple elimination and round robin, respectively. In round robin, one loss can actually deprive an entry of the league championship, if that loss is to an entry that goes through the schedule undefeated. In triple elimination, an entry must lose three times before being eliminated, and the structure allows for a second and third chance at the same opponent. Thus, close losses and upsets can be vindicated more assuredly in triple elimination than in round robin. Also, it is plausible that forfeits are less likely to occur in a situation where an entry knows that a realistic chance at gaining the championship exists, even after two losses, than in a league where two losses (and certainly three or four) practically eliminates one from championship contention.

Round robin play cannot always be considered as being a better alternative to triple elimination, or double elimination, for that matter. The one big disadvantage with triple elimination compared to round robin must be noted. As the number of entries decreases, the two tournaments become increasingly disparate with regards to the number of games involved in the tournaments and the number of time periods required to play those games. It has already been cited that, for N = 12, a triple elimination tournament has thirty-five contests and a round robin (2 leagues of six) tournament has thirty-one contests. With four contests being available for play each time period, the triple elimination tournament takes fourteen time periods to play, while round robin play only takes nine time periods.

When N = 30, and four games can be played per time period, triple elimination requires eighty-nine games and twenty-eight time periods to play. Round robin (2 leagues of eight, 2 leagues of seven) requires ninety-eight games and twenty-seven time periods. One must be aware of the fact that those comparisons are not absolute. The number of time periods required to play the tournaments can be substantially altered by changing the games available per time period and the league structures. Compared to triple elimination, round robin play becomes more efficient and/or less time-consuming as the number of games per time period increases and/or the number of leagues is increased with a corresponding decrease in the number of entries per league.

In the vast majority of cases, triple elimination requires more time periods to play than round robin, although the difference becomes less marked as the number of entries increases. Its use might be most appropriate with a moderate to large number of entries in an individual or dual competition.

In situations where every round can be played in a rather short period of time, the continual randomization elimination tournament offers two clearly desirable features. The design of the tournament virtually eliminates the possibility of forfeits, and play areas can be used to their maximal extent. Except for the possibility of having one bye in any one round, those people who appear for play *do* play. Its use is mostly geared to the one-day or short-term tournament or to tournaments held in physical education classes, where students periodically do not come to class. Sports that are not overly strenuous, and whose matches do not take a long time to play (table tennis checkers, volleyball, one-on-one basketball) are particularly appropriate for continual randomization play. The structure can also be used for a more strenuous activity, such as wrestling, in which no more than one round of matches is scheduled per day. The typically short duration of wrestling matches usually allows for completion of each round in a short time period, thus people do not have to wait too long before wrestling. If the number of entries is too large, the weight classes could be divided, such that people in the first several classes are scheduled for a specific hour, the next several classes for a later hour, and so forth.

The disadvantages are minor. All entries must be present for the drawing of matches at the start of each round. Then, some people must wait before their particular contests can be played. Some time must be consumed between rounds for the actual draw. Also, there is no provision for seeding entries.

Consolation tournaments, such as the Types I and II, are designed to provide extra play for first-game losers. Each entry is assured of playing at least two contests; however, there is no chance at winning the championship once a loss is incurred. Since the consolation brackets are of minimal significance, beyond the participation aspect, they are susceptible to forfeits by those entries who are interested only in winning the championship. However, the winner of the consolation bracket in Type II can be considered as the third-place finisher. Both consolations fit into circumstances between single and double elimination tournaments, as far as time periods to play are concerned.

When it is important to establish the most legitimate second and third-place finishers in an elimination tournament, the Bagnall-Wild structure might be appropriate. It is most suitable for situations in which time and limited participant interest and availability are not factors. The tournament structure creates several potential difficulties. Since all entries who have lost must wait for completion of the championship bracket before it is determined who plays next and who does not, one-game losers might forfeit remaining contests because they do not want to wait for any length of time to play again. The larger the number of entries, the longer the wait. In the other tournaments, losers are immediately injected into the consolation brackets. Further, there is no guarantee that every entry plays more than once. The tournament is recommended for use only when dealing with a small number of entries.

The Mueller-Anderson Playback tournament provides an adequate method for place-ranking all entries. Beyond that, its features are similar to other consolation tournaments.

In almost all circumstances, round robin tournaments guarantee the most contests per entry, because each entry plays each other entry. As previously mentioned, though, the structure is susceptible to forfeits late in the schedule, when it becomes apparent to many entries that there is no chance at winning the league championship. That possibility can be countered by manipulating league sizes. The smaller the league, the fewer contests per entry, and the fewer opportunities each entry has to forfeit. Past participation habits of a school population will influence adjustments in league size for the purposes of either increasing participation opportunities or reducing forfeit occurrences.

In previous discussion, it was mentioned that round robin play might not provide the best structure for determining a champion because an entry with only one loss could come in second to an undefeated entry. The playing of a double round robin could alleviate that problem. Also, playoff systems could be utilized whereby other entries, besides the league winners, can advance beyond league play.

Because of the many opportunities for participation, round robin play is most suitable for team sports. The large number of participants involved in each contest makes the large commitment in facility use more justifiable than for individual/dual play.

Round robin is particularly useful for outdoor sports. Contests postponed due to inclement weather need not be played the following day, but may be replayed on the first convenient date. A complete schedule, with all dates and times firmly established, may be mimeographed for distribution.

Ladder tournament structures are useful for any number of reasons and situations. They provide for play over any length of time (however long participants sustain interest), and no one is eliminated from play at any point, except by voluntary withdrawal. A major advantage and disadvantage is that the structure and scheduling can be self-administered by the participants.

That takes a burden off the sports director, but the consequent absence of central direction might lead to a tournament's eventual collapse, because opponents are not following through on their scheduling obligations. Further, participant interest may wane when the tournament reaches the point where the players get somewhat locked into relative positions, such that the same people are playing each other too often. To some extent, such an occurrence can be delayed by initially placing the best players at the bottom of the ladder.

Because of the self-administered aspect of the structure, ladder tournaments are best suited for individual and dual sports.

WHEN PEOPLE ARE SCHEDULED FOR PLAY

Three things must be established: the times of the year, the days of the week, and the times of the day that activities will be scheduled. Those may be affected by so many variables and combinations of variables that it is nearly fruitless to detail specifics. Each school's circumstances present a unique situation; at any particular school, a number of scheduling systems can be equally effective. The sports director must identify those factors that affect the content and conduct of the program and arrive at a viable scheduling pattern.

Decisions might be based on any number of the following factors: tradition, weather, interests of participants, academic calendar, conflicts with other facility users, conflicts with other school activities, conflicts with social and community events, availability of outdoor lighting, times of sunrise and sunset, meal times, classes, sleeping times, exam periods, sources of officials and supervisors, availability of participants, and so forth.

One of the most limiting aspects is to bind oneself to tradition or personal experience. All possibilities must be listed and considered. It may very well be advantageous to schedule certain sports out of their normal seasonal patterns, when facilities and varsity athletes for officiating become more available for employment in the program. Although events are most commonly scheduled Mondays through Thursdays, the other three days of the week might be usable in certain circumstances and for certain activities

The times of the day in which events can be scheduled present, perhaps, the most difficult problem, particularly for the public schools. The time period directly after school is probably the most desirable, but varsity sports usually occupy the facilities. Alternatives include the early morning, before regular school activities start, the homeroom/activity period, any free time directly before or after lunch, evenings, and weekends. At some schools, the transportation problem has been solved by altering bus schedules to accommodate intramural participants. Most collegiate intramural programs conduct events in the evenings, since much of the school population resides on or near campus.

At the beginning of each semester or term, the first week is almost necessarily devoted to an entry period, and the active part of the program can be at a standstill. Two things might be done to make those periods more useful. While entries are being taken, facilities can be opened for free play or practices. Also, a sports schedule (basketball, for instance) can be started late in one semester, and continued during the first week of the next semester. That procedure is most applicable in schools that have stable student bodies, where the vast majority of students that attends the first semester returns for the second. There is a certain risk, however, that the people who play on the first few days of the second semester will forget about their scheduled games. Precautionary phone calls could be made to team captains immediately upon their return to school. To allow time for that, the continued schedule should not start until the second school day.

A two-semester sport schedule might prove to be a problem with collegiate programs that have a large number of independent teams. The potential instability of the memberships of independent teams can easily lead to disbandment, if several players do not return to school for the following semester. Programs at commuter schools are particularly susceptible to that factor, because the number of independent teams is large, and many students do not attend school for consecutive semesters. It may be wise, therefore, to end all sports schedules within the semesters that they begin.

WHO PLAYS WHOM

People must be categorized for play in two ways — team formation and division formation. Who is eligible to play on particular teams, and which types of people and teams play each other? In answering those questions, many variables come into play, again. People and categories may be classified by gender (male, female, co-ed), physical characteristics (age, height, weight, disability), skill level (established by player preference or past performance), school circumstances (homerooms, sections, grades, bus routes, undergraduate students, graduate students, faculty, staff), and social/living circumstances (dormitory, fraternity, sorority, club, neighborhood, interest groups).

The objectives of the program must be considered. Positive sociability, competitive equality, and stability of participation are objectives that should influence decisions on who plays whom. Common bonds among players are an important factor, because they contribute to communication easements, both within the team and from sports staff to the team. That, in turn, favors positive team stability, which is very important for the stability of a program.

Some classification examples are described below.

(1) Play takes place between members of homerooms. Only those members of a particular homeroom may represent that homeroom in team or indi-

vidual competition. Males play males, females play females, and co-ed teams play co-ed teams. Comparable organization can be structured for dormitories, fraternities/sororities, grades, and the like.

(2) People who have no organizational affiliation can form teams among themselves, or have teams formed for them through random assignment or a pick-up process.

(3) Competition for certain sports, such as football and wrestling, can be categorized by weight classes, and specific basketball leagues can have height limitations.

(4) Skill level and/or attitude toward play can be the basis for forming A, B, and C leagues or divisions. The A League might include those people who choose to compete for championships at the highest level. The B League could be for players of lesser ability who want championship competition. The C League could offer purely recreational play, with no significance attached to winning or losing beyond the game itself.

FORFEITS

Forfeits are to be avoided like the plague, because they can kill a program. They tend to snowball in a tournament when participants who appear for scheduled contests for which the opponents do not show subsequently forfeit future contests for lack of interest in winning merely by forfeit. It is very frustrating for people to appear for games, sometimes under trying circumstances (bad weather, exams), only to have the other team or individual forfeit.

Several policies and procedures can be implemented to reduce forfeits. (1) In devising the entry process, separate the interested people from the more casual by making them put forth some money and effort in order to enter. Do not take entries over the phone, and establish at least a token entry fee. A forfeit fee could be collected at entry time, and returned upon completion of all schedule commitments. (2) Do not allow groups or individuals, who have forfeited an unacceptable number of past contests, to enter subsequent ones. (3) After a team has forfeited a contest, call the captain and determine the reason for the forfeit, and find out if the team intends to meet the remainder of its schedule. Explain the adverse effects that forfeits have on the program. If a team can no longer be fielded, two things can be done. The resulting gaps in the schedule can be used to reschedule postponed games; or, a team that missed the entry deadline (keep a list of them) can be substituted into the schedule, and it would assume the record of the dropped team. That policy might disgruntle those teams that would prefer winning by forfeit, as did at least one other team in the league, rather than playing the newcomer, but participation must be considered more important. (4) Automatically drop a team from the schedule after one or two forfeits. One forfeit might be permitted, because there are times when even very interested participants cannot make scheduled contests for legitimate reasons. When no forfeits are allowed, that might "force" people to play when they really should not. Teams that are dropped from play should be officially notified by phone or letter. That might prevent future confusion. (5) For elimination tournaments, which involve individual play, players may be substituted for those who do not appear for their first matches. It might be good policy to get the approval of the opponent, first. Beyond the first match, no substitutions can be made. Further, the switching of positions on a bracket should not be allowed. (6) Determine and distribute only the first two rounds of a team sport schedule. Drop those teams that forfeit. Complete the scheduling process, eliminating those pairings that involved the dropped teams, unless other teams are substituted. If no substitutions are made, those teams that would have played dropped teams later in the schedule are awarded forfeit victories for those games. (7) When a point system is in operation, impose a point penalty. Those points that would have been gained by meeting all schedule commitments could be lost; or points could be subtracted from an organization's current total. (8) Establish a ten-minute grace period beyond the time of a scheduled contest, within which an individual or team may appear without forfeiting. Beyond that time, a forfeit could be declared if the minimum number of players necessary to form a team is not present. A strict policy discourages a relaxed attitude toward having sufficient players for a full team. Games played with under-manned teams tend to be sloppy and one-sided. On the other hand, the importance of participation may be more significant than that. If so, teams or individuals arriving past the forfeit time may be allowed to play if (a) the other team or player agrees, (b) the late player or team accepts a handicap (point imposition), and (c) the playing time is altered to conform to the allotted time for the game.

POSTPONEMENTS

Postponements of scheduled contests should be granted sparingly and only under certain conditions. Otherwise, a lenient postponement policy could easily lead to frivolous requests, and established schedules would almost lose their meaning. Due to ineffective communication, postponed games can result in confusion and disputes over improper notification of teams, and further rescheduling might be necessary. Also, officiating schedules might have to be altered, and a situation may develop where officials are paid twice for the same game — once for the original gap in the schedule, and again for the actual playing of the game.

Upon mutual consent of the teams or individuals involved, the following policies could be implemented: (1) Postponements are granted if teams or individuals play on their own time, without assigned officials, and as long as the flow of the schedule is not interrupted or held back. (2) Officiated games are rescheduled only within the regular daily sequence and only when a gap in the schedule exists due to a known, upcoming forfeit.

Whenever games are postponed due to inclement weather, they may be rescheduled on weekends or at the end of the regular season. Although the participation emphasis of sports would be compromised, it might be expeditious to reschedule for the end of the season only those games that affect the determination of league champions.

MANIPULATING CONTEST LENGTH

Predictable contest length is a very important aspect of scheduling. In most sports programs, more than one contest must be scheduled per play area per day. Administrative efficiency and, thereby, participant satisfaction, can be enhanced when contests can be scheduled and played such that they almost always start and finish as expected.

The nature of an activity can largely dictate how much time must be allotted for the completion of a scheduled contest. Match lengths for such sports as tennis, badminton, and handball are not regulated by time limits, so an estimate of the average time required to complete a contest must be made for scheduling purposes. However, there are many sports that can be subjected to time limits; to the extent possible, their rules should be modified so contests can typically be completed in fifty minutes. That allows a ten-minute period for players of the preceding game to leave the play area, and players of the following game to be organized for play. Then, contests can be scheduled on an hourly basis. Modifications of sports rules are discussed in books on Intramural Sports.

OVERSCHEDULING AND UNDERSCHEDULING

Point systems influence organizations to coerce people to participate in activities in which they have little interest, or at times that conflict with activities that are really more important (schoolwork, for example). The number of times per week that an individual might be "forced" or subconsciously influenced to participate in sports should be limited, so that individual can attend to other concerns of life. That should be a scheduling consideration whether or not a point system is operative. It may be wise, therefore, to limit the scheduling of individuals or teams to no more than twice per week.

Along similar lines, officials and supervisory staff should not be overscheduled. Further, the *daily* supply of officials and supervisory staff must be considered when scheduling. Even if an unlimited number of play areas were available, the number of available officials and supervisory staff would limit play.

For certain team sports, the number of entries and consequent league structures may be such that the normal scheduling pattern requires alteration. The number of total games to be scheduled may exceed what was anticipated or, at the opposite extreme, the number of total games is less than anticipated. Some choices must be made regarding the addition or subtraction of those games from the predetermined days and times of day set aside for scheduling use. Whole days of play can be added or subtracted, or time slots may be added or subtracted across all play areas. In so doing, the availability and daily workload of officials and supervisors must be considered, as well as the administrative efficiency of their use.

For example, if the normal scheduling sequence uses three time periods per play area per day, and games must be added, one must choose between the alternatives of adding a fourth time period per play area for as many days as necessary (Can the officials be expected to handle an extra game per day effectively?), adding an undesirable day of the week (Friday, for example) for as many weeks as necessary, or adding extra normal scheduling days (Monday through Thursday) to the end of the anticipated last day of the season. Other factors influence that decision-making process, and similar considerations affect choices to be made when games must be subtracted. For the latter circumstance, it is probably most efficient to lower the number of days used, and maintain the normal number of time periods per day.

Whenever the numbers of play areas and time periods exceed what can be used per day, a choice must be made between increasing the use of play areas and reducing the number of time periods, or retaining the number of time periods and reducing the play areas used. Assuming that enough officials are available, the former alternative improves supervisory efficiency, because the total daily time over which sports are conducted is reduced. If the availability of officials is questionable, the latter alternative improves the efficiency of the employment of officials, because fewer officials are required to cover a fewer number of play areas.

A situation may occur where a tremendous increase in the number of total games to be scheduled requires an increase in both the days and time periods used. If a sufficient supply of officials exists, two shifts of officials could be scheduled to cover a day's schedule of games on each play area. For instance, one set of officials works the first three games, and a second set works the last several games.

CONFLICTS

Prior to scheduling, the different areas of conflicts that people might have with the scheduled times of play must be considered. Tournament directors should make notes (on a calendar, perhaps) of all official schoolwide activities, social functions of special groups, community-related events, and the influence of television. In other words, what might people rather be doing on particular days than participating in sports?

Beyond that, potential conflicts among activities within the program must be identified. Quite commonly, more than one sport activity occurs simultaneously. One must be careful not to schedule badminton play for the same hours and play areas on which basketball is also scheduled. If different activities are scheduled sequentially on the same play area or concurrently on different play areas, the availability of supervisors, officials, and the participants, themselves, must be noted. It is particularly easy to forget that many individuals are members of more than one team within a sport (where coed teams exist) and participate on teams of sports that are concurrently conducted. As noted in the chapter on the entry process, information should be requested from team captains as to the other teams on which a significant number of teammates play, so scheduling conflicts may be avoided. Also, when the seasons of several team sports overlap, it may be beneficial to afford team captains, at time of entry, the opportunity to indicate accurately the times in which their teams cannot play due to schedule commitments in another sport(s). That is possible if entry deadlines are staggered so the schedule of one sport is distributed before the entry deadline of the next sport.

Scheduling techniques can be devised for automatic avoidance of direct conflicts. For instance, coed play can be scheduled on days or times of day that no other division of play in that sport is scheduled. While that would eliminate direct conflicts, one must be wary of indirect conflicts. Individuals should not be expected to play a game at 8:00 PM in the male division and a co-ed game at 9:00 PM. In that regard, particular attention should be paid to strenuous sports. Softball and volleyball are two team sports that could be played back-to-back without much difficulty.

COMMUNICATION OF SCHEDULES

Essentially, there are four ways to communicate schedules.
(1) They may be printed in quantity, and mailed to participants. This, perhaps, is the most efficient method, although a several-day gap exists between the entry deadline and start of play, because schedules must be formulated, typed, mimeographed, put into envelopes, mailed, and delivered.
(2) Rather than mail printed schedules, they may be picked up in the sports office at a specific time by team captains or individual players. That saves the cost of mailing and the time taken for mail delivery, but the procedure lacks consistency of communication. Some people pick up schedules on time, and some do not; some never do pick them up. The sports staff must then make telephone calls to delinquent participants, or otherwise get the schedules to them. A policy could be instituted whereby people delinquent in picking up schedules are immediately dropped, and people or teams on a waiting list are substituted.
(3) Schedules could be typed in single copy, run through a copy machine, and posted in appropriate places around school. To indicate which in-

dividuals or team captains have seen the schedule, a check mark beside a person's name or team could be made on the schedule posted in the intramural office. This procedure poses advantages and disadvantages similar to those indicated immediately above.

(4) Along with posting schedules, they could be recorded on a device that is connected to a special telephone line. Anyone wishing to know what the next several days' schedule of games is need only dial a number that connects to the special telephone line. The installation of such a line is rather expensive, and a new recording must be made every time a day's play is completed, which could be almost every day. However, the convenience the system would provide participants may make the financial expenditure and effort worthwhile.

REFERENCE

Fabian, Lou. "Scheduling Intramural Programs for Commuter Colleges," *Journal of the National Intramural-Recreational Sports Association*, 2:49-52, May, 1978.